The Ebony Treasure Map

The Roadmap To Riches
For African Americans

Myron Golden

Published by
Myron Golden Enterprises

The Ebony Treasure Map

Copyright © 2006 Myron Golden Enterprises

All rights reserved. No part of this book may be reproduced in any form except for the inclusion of brief quotations in review, without the express written permission of Myron Golden and Myron Golden Enterprises.

ISBN: 0-9788944-0-5

Printed in the U.S. By Instant Publisher.

The Ebony Treasure Map

Acknowledgements

This book is dedicated to my parents, James and Carolyn Golden who encouraged me and started telling me at a young age that I could do anything. I sure am glad I believed them. It is dedicated to my wife Tonie Golden, who is the inspiration for all of my accomplishments. I dedicate it to my children; Adam, A.C. and Dee Dee Golden who have given me a reason to be a good example and helped me to grow in ways that I wouldn't have realized were necessary. I dedicate it to my mentor and friend Jerry Clark for sharing his wealth of knowledge, experience and friendship with me. I dedicate it to all of my students who have proven the validity of the principles I teach by the results they have produced. I dedicate it to my six brothers Jeff Golden, Pastor Michael Golden, Rob Golden, Dwayne Golden, Derrick Golden and Marc Golden. I dedicate it to my Mother-In-Law Patsy Williams who prays for me and is one of my dearest friends. I dedicate it to all of my family members, aunts, uncles, in-laws, cousins, nieces and nephews. I also give grateful acknowledgements to my editor Lauren Hidden for her untiring work and patience with me during this book project. I also have to acknowledge some of my other mentors, David Mitchell, and Ben Ginder; these are some of my millionaire mentors who impacted my life early and assisted me on my journey. Finally I have to acknowledge my nephew Daniel Golden for the design of the book cover; for having patience with me for all the demands placed on him during this project.

The Ebony Treasure Map

Table Of Contents

Forward by Jerry "Drhino" Clark

Introduction — 1

CHAPTER ONE:

What Are Your Chances Of Becoming Rich? — 6

CHAPTER TWO:

The Difference Between The Rich And The Poor — 10

CHAPTER THREE:

The Window Of Opportunity — 21

CHAPTER FOUR:

What Kind Of House Do You Live In? — 30

CHAPTER FIVE:

The Hands Free Money Business Plan — 51

CHAPTER SIX:

All Businesses Are Not Created Equal — 54

CHAPTER SEVEN:

Leverage Your Business Through Technology — 58

CHAPTER EIGHT:

It's Better To Be A V.M. Than It Is To Be A V.P. — 66

The Ebony Treasure Map

CHAPTER NINE:

Know What Business You're Really In — 74

CHAPTER TEN:

Find A Treasure Guide Who
Has Already Found The Treasure — 78

CHAPTER ELEVEN:

You Have No Competition — 81

CHAPTER TWELVE:

Since You Can't Beat 'Em, Join 'Em — 85

CHAPTER THIRTEEN:

You Can If Your Cans Say You Can — 86

CHAPTER FOURTEEN:

13 Mental Treasure Traps That
Can Keep You From Your Treasure — 93

CHAPTER FIFTEEN:

Thirteen Practical Treasure Traps
That Can Keep You From Your Treasure — 126

CHAPTER SIXTEEN:

How To Get Started On The Road To Riches — 135

About The Author — 134

The Ebony Treasure Map

Forward

I remember driving down the highway with my Mother when all of a sudden a beautiful Candy Apple Red Automobile gracefully glided past us… I was 11 years of age and I had never seen a Car like that. I asked my Mother, "What type of Car is that?" She said that it was a Mercedes Benz. I then asked her why we didn't have a Car like that. She looked at me and said, because she didn't go to school and get a good education and get a good job like the guy who was driving the Mercedes did.

From that point onward, I committed to following the treasure map that my mom had laid out for me. However, after years and years of doing well in school and getting a good job, I came across a startling realization: The treasure map that was given to me by my mom was a map that was empty of treasure… It was a harsh discovery for me, and at the same time, it was life changing.

This experience was life changing because it caused me to take some time to pause and think. I thought, "If I'm going to get a treasure map, wouldn't it be smart to get one from someone who has been a proven guide to the discovery of treasure?" The answer for me was a resounding "yes"! From that point on, I vowed to seek guides that could provide treasure maps that they have already proven in their lives have true treasure… Myron Golden is such a Guide – and a highly effective one at that.

The Ebony Treasure Map

I am very excited about the book you now hold in your hands – The Ebony Treasure Map – and I'm even more excited knowing what kind of life experience you will create if you follow the principles and strategies presented within this book.

Being raised an African American in the inner city ghettos – I now realize that the best thing my mother could have done for me when I was 11 years of age and wanted to know how to go about getting a Mercedes Benz and creating a life of abundance would have been to give me a copy of this book...

Oops... There was only one problem – this book wasn't written then... But now it is and you have a unique benefit that I didn't have... My desire is that you dedicate at least 30-60 minutes per day not only reading – but implementing the processes that Myron Golden teaches you in this book. Myron walks his talk. I have personally seen him use the exact information that he will be teaching you in this book to go from the Depths of Despair to the Peaks of Prosperity...

By the way, after finding successful Treasure Maps and Treasure Guides (at the age of 18), I was able to purchase my First Mercedes Benz when I was 19 years old, and I'm now a Multi-Millionaire ☺

Understand that the information in this Book is information that only "an elite few" have, understand,

and implement. You now have an opportunity to join that group…

Are you ready for the Journey?

Ok, then come on and open up this map and let's go get some Treasure…

Go, Go, Go!!!

Jerry "DRhino" Clark
www.clubrhino.com

The Ebony Treasure Map

Introduction

Thank you for taking the time to read this book. Before we dive into reading "The Ebony Treasure Map," you should know that this book is absolutely necessary to the financial future of black people in America and all over the world. The principles in the Ebony Treasure Map will work for people of any race, but I believe that we African Americans deserve to have a financial book written just for us by one of us, so that each of us can help all of us. This book had to be written by someone who is practicing the principles of wealth and prosperity. Today's marketplace holds too much information produced by those who have only theories and no practical experience. I have no untested theories for you in this book. I only have practical advice that I have personally used to bring me from the pit of poverty to the peak of prosperity.

I want to start out by telling you my story, so you can be encouraged and challenged.

I was born in a segregated hospital in Tampa, Florida in 1961. The conditions in the hospital were so poor that I contracted polio soon after my birth. My parents knew that something was wrong with me, but it wasn't until months later, when we moved to Pennsylvania that I was diagnosed and treated for polio.

Polio affected my left leg: it left me with partial paralysis and atrophy. Because of this, I have always walked with a brace on my leg. From the time I started to grow, my left leg was shorter than my right. By the time I was 13 years old my left leg was two inches shorter. So I had to wear orthopedic shoes (one of the shoes had a two inch soul). As you can imagine, when I was a young child, I was teased a lot.

When I was thirteen years old, the doctors came to my parents and said, "Mr. and Mrs. Golden, we believe that we have an operation that will help your son. We can stretch his leg two inches." I can remember thinking to myself that it sounded kind of crazy— to stretch a leg with a bone in it. The doctor explained how he would have to break my leg and I would be in the hospital for a month. I was very excited about this because it meant that I didn't have to go to school for a whole month. My parents and I agreed to the surgical procedure. So they broke my tibia in the middle and the fibula at the top and the bottom. They put screws through my leg and attached the screws to an apparatus. They turned the knobs on the apparatus every day. At the end of thirty days, my leg was stretched two inches.

The leg-stretch operation worked. Even though I still wear a brace on my leg, I don't have to wear orthopedic shoes anymore—I don't have to wear one shoe with a thick sole and one shoe with a regular sole.

In addition to the challenges I faced with my leg, I was the second of seven brothers and I basically grew up poor. My parents were hardworking people who did the best they could, but they didn't really understand how money works.

I, too, didn't understand how money worked. Having this lack of understanding presented me with some challenges as a young adult struggling to make a living. As you can imagine, having a physical challenge makes it somewhat difficult to get a job. So, when I got married, I was still poor. My wife is a beautiful woman

The Ebony Treasure Map

and I made her a lot of promises, but I didn't know how to keep them. I can remember being so broke at one point that my wife and I were actually taking all of the cushions off of the furniture and the seats out of the car, looking for pennies to buy a loaf of bread, so we could make peanut butter and jelly sandwiches. We were really poor. In fact, when my wife was eight months pregnant with our first child, the electricity and water in our house were shut off at the same time. When my first son was born, we actually had to go on welfare for a few months, for the medical benefits because we didn't have insurance to cover his birth.

About a month later, I got a job driving a trash truck. I was earning $6.25 an hour. Each day, I drove four or five trash trucks to the dump and emptied them. I'd wake up at two-thirty in the morning, go to that cold, dark truck yard and check the oil, hydraulics and tire pressure, and then start driving the trucks to the dump to empty them. I would usually make about four to five trips per day. However, on my breaks, and when my truck was stuck in traffic, I would read personal development books. I turned my truck into a university on wheels, because I was always listening to educational, inspirational, motivational, and, most of all, transformational tapes. Driving a trash truck was just a job to make enough money to almost support my family. I realized even then that poverty and being a trash man was not my destiny. It was the place where God was getting me ready for what he already had ready for me.

Eventually, I was promoted to a salesperson and started selling trash removal services to businesses. At the same time, I started running a business out of my home. At first, my home business didn't do so well because I didn't know how to run a business. I had spent my entire working life learning how to be an employee. I had a few jobs after "the trash man" job. Eventually, my home business did so well that I was able to walk away from having a job. From then on, I knew I would never again work for anyone else, trading time for money.

When I first got started in a home-based business in 1985, even though I was really horrible at it, the experience was invaluable. Because of the principles that I learned in home-based business, I now earn more on a monthly basis than the average person in America earns in a year. I have had experiences where I have earned more in a day, even more in an hour, than the average person in this country makes in two years. I now earn more on a monthly basis than I earned in the entire decade of the eighties. I don't tell you this to impress you, but to impress upon you that if I can have this kind of radical income growth, then you can experience similar results.

Despite the success I now experience, I know what it's like to be poor. This is not a book written by someone who was born with a silver spoon in his mouth. This is not a book written by someone who has had all of the great breaks in life. This is a book written by someone just like you, someone who has had big and small challenges. However, I've figured out a way to overcome those challenges and become wealthy in the wealthiest country that has ever existed on the face of the earth.

This book, "The Ebony Treasure Map," is filled with principles that can make you richer than you ever thought you could be. Some people may wonder, "Why do you have to have a special book on financial independence just for black people? Won't the same principles work for everybody?"

The answer is "yes" and "no." In fact, the same principles that help white people, Asian people or Spanish people become wealthy will help black people become wealthy, as well. However, there are some unique perceptions black people have that must be addressed in order for black people to avoid some pitfalls that are particular to our ethnic group. If we don't change some of our beliefs and perceptions, they can literally hinder us from ever reaching the financial goal of becoming rich in the richest country that has ever existed on the face of the earth.

If you follow "The Ebony Treasure Map," you will find your treasure at the end of this financial journey. Though many people believe it's not possible for a black person to be successful in America because of the establishment, they're wrong. I can show you the path in the "Ebony Treasure" and how to finish rich.

CHAPTER ONE

What Are Your Chances of Becoming Rich?

Back in the 1980's, I sold insurance. At that time, the insurance company that I represented used Social Security Administration data that showed how the average person ends up after working a lifetime in America. I believe the statistics would be the same today, if not much worse. You don't want to be on the bottom half of these statistics.

Here are the statistics: of 100 people working from age 20 to age 65 (a 45-year time period), one becomes rich, four become financially independent, five are still working, 28 are dead, and 62 are dead broke. Let's look at this according to percentages.

What that means is this: in America, 5% of the people make it financially, and 95% don't. That's an amazing statistic.

There's a definite line that separates the "haves" from the "have nots" when it comes to making it financially in America. Five percent make it. Ninety-five percent don't. That's scary when you think about it. It's even scarier when you read those numbers in a bit of a different way. In the wealthiest country that has ever existed in the history of the world, you have a 95% chance of not making it and only a 5% shot at making it.

Among black people, the percentage of people that don't make it is probably worse. It might be 97% of the people don't make it and 3% make it. Why? Because we don't have parents and grandparents who talk to their children and grandchildren about how money works. Therefore, a larger percentage of our people don't understand how money works and how to make money work for us. By the time you're done reading this book, however, you'll have the tools to become financially independent. You will also have the wherewithal to teach your children and grandchildren these principles and change your family for generations.

When you think about the fact that 5% of the people make it and 95% don't make it, how does that make you feel? Does it make you feel afraid? Does it make you feel concerned? Does it make you feel angry? Does it make you feel slighted? Does it make you wonder which one of those two groups you are in? If it does, that's good. If it doesn't, then this book probably won't help you.

Since you are reading this book, I'll assume that you're a person who has a desire to end up in the top 5% instead of the bottom 95%. If I have pegged you right, and you are one of the people who want to be in the 5%, I can tell you how to do it in two sentences. In fact, these two sentences are so simple and so powerful that, if you follow them, they will make you rich.

Before we get into that, however, I want to make sure you are ready for your "life change" and that you are open to ideas that will challenge your thinking. That's exactly what this book will do. It's going to give you some great ideas to think about. It's going to give you some steps to take on your journey to becoming wealthy in the wealthiest country that has ever existed. I want you to realize from the beginning that nothing in this book is status quo, and it will challenge your thinking. But remember this—while these concepts are

The Ebony Treasure Map

more than likely to be "outside the box" for you, consider this, if your way of thinking could make you rich, you would already be there, or on your way there. With that in mind, let's look at the "Two-Sentence Wealth Formula".

Out of 100 people who work from age 20 to age 65, these are the statistics of how they end up 45 years later.

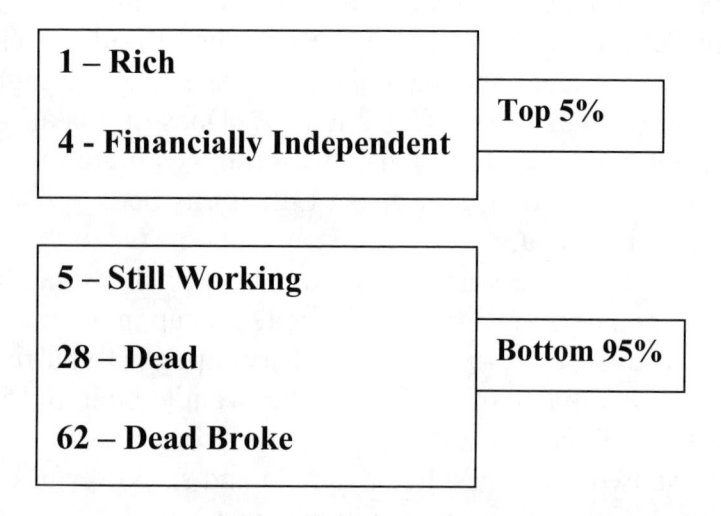

1 – Rich	
4 - Financially Independent	Top 5%

5 – Still Working	
28 – Dead	Bottom 95%
62 – Dead Broke	

    The Two-Sentence Wealth Formula is this: "If you want to become wealthy, then you have to find out what the top 5% of people do financially and do the same thing." That is sentence number one. The second sentence in The Two-Sentence Wealth Formula is even more important than the first: "You've got to find out what the bottom 95% are doing financially and, whatever else you do, don't do what they do."
    The question then remains, "What do the top 5% do, that the bottom 95% don't do? What do the bottom 95% do that the top 5% don't do?" You need to study these two

things in great detail. I would recommend that you become fanatical about finding out the difference between the habits of the rich and the habits of the poor. If you study both wealth and poverty, you can learn how to become wealthy. Write down what you learn and follow it to the letter.

As simple and as funny as these two sentences might seem, most people never do either one. In the first part of this book, I'll show you how to make a list and start studying wealth and poverty, so that you can understand what the differences are. Then you will be able to make a conscious decision to become wealthy.

Also know that every financial principle I teach in this book is based on Biblical principles. I understand that most people think that it's God's design for them to be broke and for them to struggle. I read in the Bible in Proverbs 10:22, which says, "The blessing of the Lord, it maketh rich, and He addeth no sorrow with it." Well, if that's the case, the question I have for you is, "Is that your experience?"

"The hand of the diligent maketh rich, but the slothful shall be under tribute." (Proverbs 12:24) That's a principle. (Diligence is more likely to bring riches and laziness is more likely to bring poverty). All principles always work the same for everybody. Follow the principles that rich people follow and stop following the principles that poor people follow, and you will become rich. It's that simple.

Let's start the list. Get out a journal or a notebook and start writing. Make two lists: one will be "What Rich People Do", and one will be "What Poor People Do." Start paying attention to the differences between the habits of the rich: and the habits of the poor and start modeling the habits of the rich immediately. In the next chapter we will begin to examine some of the differences between the habits of the rich and the habits of the poor.

CHAPTER TWO

The Difference Between The Rich And The Poor

Rich people understand how money works. Poor people only understand how to work for money. Let me say that again. Rich people understand how money works, but poor people only understand how to work for money. You may be wondering, "Myron, what do you mean 'understand how money works?'" Let me explain.

The Importance of Financial Principles

Any financial principle that you do not understand, and any financial principle you are not using, is being used against you by someone who does understand that principle. That's why it's so important for you to understand financial principles.

Most people don't understand any financial principles. They don't understand leverage. They don't understand residual income. They don't understand passive income. They don't understand "the time value of money". They don't understand the power of compound interest. Their lack of knowledge about how most financial principles work is the reason they are broke. Let's look at some financial principles and how they work (for you if you understand them and use them, and against you if you don't).

The Magic of Compound Interest

Rich people understand the time value of money. They understand the value of compound interest. Einstein, who is considered to be one of the brightest people of the last century said, "Compound interest is the most powerful force in the universe."

I want you to think about that statement: if compound interest is the most powerful force in the universe, you need to understand it. If you don't understand it, someone who does will use the most powerful financial force in the universe against you. You can see how this could easily have a catastrophic affect on your financial situation.

Einstein, the same guy who discovered that $E=MC^2$ and unlocked the secrets to the atom bomb, said that compound interest is more powerful than the force that results in an atomic explosion. If that is true, no wonder so many people end up broke. Institutions that understand compound interest are using that force against you, financially.

Let me show you how. You put your money in a bank account that will give you less than 3%, sometimes even less than 1% interest on your money. Then you get a credit card through the same bank and you borrow your own money from the bank at 18%-24% interest. No wonder most people are broke. They loan their money to the bank at 0%-3% interest and borrow it back at 18%-24%. To see the affect this could have on you financially over a working lifetime, let's use the "Rule of 72".

The rule of 72 is the formula that measures compound interest (also known as the time value of money). Here's how it works: take your rate of return and divide it by the number 72. The answer tells you how long it will take your money to double at that rate of return. For example, 72 divided by 3 equals 24. That tells you that if you are getting a 3% return on your money; your money will double every 24 years. If you reverse that equation and you're getting 24% on your money, then your money will double every 3 years. That is why your bank is getting richer at your expense. They know this formula and you don't. Now you can clearly see why most people never get rich. You must commit to getting your money working for you at the highest rates of return possible (by the way, rate of return simply means interest).

That's why poor people are poor and rich people are rich. Rich people know this system doesn't work to their advantage.

Now let's continue looking at the differences between the practices of the rich and the practices of the poor.

Don't Work for Money, Have Money Work For You
Poor people only understand how to work for money. What do I mean? Many poor people are hard-working individuals who have a job that they either classify as a good job or a bad job. Let me tell you, a job is a job. Some jobs pay more money than others, but it doesn't change the fact that you are trading time for money. The reason people work for money is that they believe that time is money. Rich people know that time is not money; time is infinitely more valuable than money. To prove it, think about this: if you run out of money, you can always get more money; but if you run out of time—it's over—you can't get more time.

Learn how to stop trading your time for money. Your employer already knows that time is more valuable than money. Even if you haven't figured it out yet. That's why you are willing to give your employer a whole lot of your time for a little bit of your employer's money.

On the other hand, because your employer understands that time is more valuable than money, the company is willing to give you a little bit of their money for a whole lot of your time. When you figure out this reality, then you will stop trading your time, which is infinitely valuable, for money, which only has a limited value. When you trade time for money, it is like renting out your life for less than it is worth. When you rent out your life over a long period of time, you sell out your family. I don't want you to go quit your job tomorrow. I do want you to begin to set up your life so that, eventually, you can put a system in place to make enough passive income to buy back your time.

Now let's look at some more differences between the rich and the poor.

Don't Entertain Yourself; Educate Yourself

Another difference between the wealthy and the poor is that poor people entertain themselves, but rich people educate themselves. Poor people collect DVDs and movies and video games. Rich people collect books, seminar experiences, and audio programs that teach them how to do something they want to learn how to do. Let me repeat. Poor people entertain themselves. Rich people educate themselves.

Poor people stop learning as soon as they get out of school. Rich people continue their education long after they graduate. In fact, most rich people will tell you that the most valuable things they have learned, they didn't learn from school anyway. They learned them from mentors. They learned them from seminars. They learned them from books. They learned them from audio programs. They learn the things they want to learn from people who know what they want to learn. Poor people entertain themselves. Rich people educate themselves. Stop entertaining yourself and start educating yourself.

Throw Away Your Television
    I believe that people who are financially challenged should not watch television until they are financially free. To me, "financially challenged" means that you are making less than $20,000 a month. If you are making less than $20,000 a month and you don't feel financially challenged, you eventually will feel challenged. Because, as your children get older and your parents get older, you will begin to experience additional responsibilities that get more expensive on both ends.

    You'll be taking care of children who are getting older, going to college and getting married. At the same time, you will have increased responsibilities with parents who are getting older. Both have increased needs. If you are making less than $20,000 a month at that point, you're going to find yourself in a financial crunch, or feeling guilty about what you wish you could do but can't.

    I realize that twenty thousand dollars a month may be hard for you to conceptualize. But twenty thousand a month will eventually seem like a little bit of money to you if you will trust the principles of this book and apply them to your life. So if you can see it, if you can believe it, then you can achieve it. You will eventually see that making $20,000 a month is not only possible, but it's very, very probable, if you follow all of the principles in this book.

Now that you are contemplating twenty thousand per month, let me tell you why I say getting rid of your television is so important. There are actually many reasons, so let's examine some of them. The television is a cultural hypnotic device. It is used to influence and control society. The programming, the news media and the commercials have a profound effect on the financial situation of most people.

The television creates a victim mentality as people watch the rapes, robberies and murders on the evening news or on violent TV dramas, they become more and more fearful. The commercials create a consumer mentality that encourages people to buy things they don't need and can't afford. TV keeps people trapped into thinking they're powerless and that changing their financial situation is impossible. The exact opposite is true. You are the one who has the best chance of changing your financial life. Not the government and not a social program.

Another problem with television is that it promotes the philosophy that the main purpose of money is consumption (or buying things), but the truth is that the more important function of money is for creating wealth.

The final argument that I will give in favor of poor people getting rid of their televisions is this: the time it takes to watch it. The average American spends 4 to 7 hours per day watching television. That valuable time could be used to learn something, or do something, that can create wealth.

When I was broke, I got rid of my television, and it was one of the best things I ever did. I can honestly tell you that getting rid of my television was one of the most important things I have ever done that has contributed to my wealth.

So get rid of your television until you get over the financial hump. Benjamin Franklin said, "If you empty your purse into your mind, your mind will fill your purse with gold."

I'm going to give you the "Myron Golden" version of that. And that is, "Whoever puts the most money in your mind, that's who has most of your money". Let me explain.

Advertisers spend millions of dollars to put messages in your mind. You cannot compete at that level, so they automatically have an advantage over you. If the advertisers put more money into your mind than you do, then the advertisers will have more of your money than you will. Because all of the money they invest in your mind causes you to think about what they want you to think about (why you should buy more of their products).

Since you can't compete at that level, you've got to cut off the advertisers, turn off the television, turn off the radio, put down the newspaper, stop reading that magazine and start focusing solely, like a fanatic, on how you are going to become financially independent.

Becoming rich can't be something that you do haphazardly. It has to be something that you are intent on making work. In order for that to happen, you've got to cut off all of those influences that are pouring more money into your mind than you are.

You may be thinking, "If I do this, how will I know what is going on in the world?" (That is exactly what they want you to think). My question is, if you can't do anything about what is going on in your own world, how are you going to do something about what is going on in "the" world?

With all of this in mind, do you think that you can still afford to watch television before you become wealthy?

Most Rich People Don't Have Jobs

Another difference between poor people and rich people is that poor people have jobs, whereas rich people own businesses. More than 80% of rich people became rich by owning their own business. Poor people seek to get a job. Rich people look to give somebody a job. Think about it: rich people value their time so much that they hire people to do the things they don't want to do. But poor people will gladly get paid to do what those of us who are rich really don't want to do.

Understand that the word "J.O.B." is the most perfectly spelled word in the dictionary, J.O.B. It is an acronym that stands for "**J**ump **O**ut of **B**ed", "get on the **J**ourney **O**f the **B**roke" so you can remain "**J**ust **O**ver **B**roke."

I want you to get to the place in your life where the word "job" makes you cringe. I hope that, by now, you don't like the idea of selling your time to somebody else, because then you are selling your most valuable asset for pennies on the dollar. Poor people seek to get a job, whereas rich people own businesses. If you want to be wealthy and own your own business or businesses, then you are starting to get the idea of this book. Later in this book I am going to share with you my business plan which has absolutely changed my life. It's so simple, even a fifth grader could understand it.

Rich People Don't Set Limits For Themselves

Poor people think "either or." Rich people think "both and". What this means is that poor people look at every choice as a process of elimination. For instance, a person might think, "I would like to do what I love, but I have to pay my bills." That statement implies that you can't have both. We buy into "truisms" that aren't true, like the saying, "You can't have your cake and eat it too". Of course you can have your cake and eat it too. How else would you eat your cake, if you didn't have it first? The actual quote is, "You can't eat your cake and have it [save it] too." Ironically, the latter statement is why poor people get poorer and rich people get richer. Rich people don't try to eat their cake and have it too.

Let me illustrate. Rich people are conservative spenders, but many poor people will spend everything they get as soon as they get it. Then they wonder why they never accumulate wealth. You see, "You can't spend your money and have it too. Too many poor people will spend more money than they should to buy things they really can't afford, to impress people that they don't know. The next time you are tempted to do this, stop and say to yourself, "I can spend this now and have nothing later, or I can invest this now and have a fortune later." "You can't eat your cake and have it too". And "you can't spend your money and have it too". If you want to be rich, you must resist the temptation to spend present cash that you could be using, and should be using to create future wealth. Once you have created your wealth, then you can become a "both and" person. Because you will then have the ability to travel wherever you choose, and you will enjoy a nice lifestyle without having to worry about money.

Poor people think "either or," but rich people think "both and". Poor people think, "Well, I've got to do either this or this." Rich people think "How can I do both?" Start changing the way you think.

Poor people focus on the obstacle. Rich people focus on the opportunity. It's all a question of focus. In every situation, there are both obstacles and opportunities, which one do you usually see?. Start thinking like a rich person and you will eventually be rich.

Choose Your Advisors Wisely

The difference that I am about to show you is one of the most ironic of all the differences between the rich and poor. Rich people only take financial advice from people who are as rich as they are or richer. Poor people only take financial advice from people who are as poor as they are or poorer. This is one of the most amazing things that I have seen since I began studying this subject. It is really sad, because most people will go to the grave and never even realize that if what they are currently doing is not giving them the result they desire, then they should start looking to some different sources for advice. One of the best definitions of insanity I have ever heard is, "continuing to do the same things and expecting a different result". If you continue to do what you have always done, then you will continue to get what you have always gotten.

Now I have given you the start to a pretty good list of differences between the rich and the poor. It is not an exhaustive list, but it is a good start. While you are on your personal wealth journey, continue to grow your list of differences between the rich and the poor and I will look forward to hearing your story one day of how you made it into the top 5%.

CHAPTER THREE

The Window Of Opportunity

The Window of Opportunity has more to do with your perspective on money and how it's made than anything else. Let me illustrate this for you.

On the next page you will see an intersection. In the center of this intersection, that "$" is where an accident happens. There are four people standing on four corners and they all see the same accident. My question to you is, "Did they all see the same thing?" The answer is, "Of course not." They all saw something different. The reason they all saw something different is because they were all looking at the situation from a different perspective. Just like this illustration about the accident, our financial life has a lot more to do with perspective than most people realize. Your perspective is critical to the results you produce in your financial life. Have you ever stopped to consider your current perspective about money? Have you ever thought about the fact you're your perspective is either keeping you from your dreams or making them a reality? If you were aware of how much power your perspective actually has, you would consciously create a perspective that serves you well and you would eliminate the ones the do not serve you well. When you finish the next two chapters, you will have a brand new perspective that can make you rich beyond your imagination. Let's look at the following illustration to see if it will clarify for us our current perspective and help us develop a new one if necessary.

The Ebony Treasure Map

We know that these four people all saw the same accident but they didn't see the same thing. Seldom do we see things the way they are. Most of the time, we see things the way we see them because of where we are. One of my purposes in writing this book is to move you to a different place in your life, so you can see things that you couldn't see before. It's not about what happens, as much as it is about how you view what happens.

Now we're going to take this intersection and turn it into a window. This window has four panes in it. So instead of saying there are four people watching an accident, we're going to say they are all looking out the window.

The Ebony Treasure Map

You may be wondering why I put a "$" there for an accident. The reason is this: if most people make any real money in their life, it's an accident. If they keep any of the money they make, that's also an accident.

Now let's draw a box around our intersection and turn our intersection into a window with 4 window panes.

The Window of Opportunity

O.A.S.	S.M.S.
:)	:)
H.A.J.	O.A.J.
:(	:(

(with "$" at the center intersection)

So we've got four people looking through the Window of Opportunity and all four of them are looking at money through that window from a different window pane; that is why they all have different perspectives.

The lower left is the H.A.J. window pane. Right beside it on the bottom right is the O.A.J. window pane. Top left is the O.A.S. window pane. The top right is the S.M.S. window pane.

Those are the window panes in the Window of Opportunity. H.A.J. is in the lower left. It is in the bottom part of the window. The reason why is because H.A.J. stands for "Have A Job".

The Worst Way To Make Money

Having A Job is, without question, the worst legitimate way to make money. Unfortunately, for most people in this country, having a job is the only way they know how to make money. Of course, if you ask people how they like their job, they often say, "Well, you have to have a job" or "I've gotta pay my bills."

Having a job is the worst way to make money, because you trade your time for money. As we've already discussed, time is more valuable than money. So you're trading something valuable for something that, at best, has a limited value.

The second reason that having a job is the worst way to make money is because you only have so much time. This means that if you have a job, you can only make so much money.

Another reason that having a job is the worst way to make money is because nobody is willing to pay you what you are worth. Think about it. Go ask 10 people that you work with, 10 people in your neighborhood, 10 people at your church, and 10 people in your family, if they feel like they are paid what they're worth. I promise you that every last one of them will tell you, "No!" They will never be paid what they are worth, working for someone else.

The Second Worst Way To Make Money

The second way to make money on the bottom right is O.A.J. That stands for Own A Job. Most people think that they are going from having a job into having their own business, but what they're really doing is going from having a job to owning a job. What owning a job means is they start a business in which they are the only employee, which means they are in high demand. They go from having one boss over in the "Have A Job" window pane to 37 bosses called customers or clients in the "Own A Job" window pane.

People who own jobs generally make more money than people who have jobs, because they decide how much they get paid and are usually in high demand. However, because they are usually the only person doing the work, they generally have less time than people who have a job. Owning a job is better than having a job because you make more money, but it's worse than having a job because it usually means you have less time.

You don't want to go from having a job to owning a job. Another really bad thing about having a job or owning a job is that it is the most risky financial situation you can put yourself or your family into. If something happens to you and you can't work, then your income comes to a screeching halt. Many people have found themselves devastated financially after becoming disabled or unemployed, because they were the only source of their income. You don't want this to happen to you and your family. One of the best things you can do is get to the point in your life where you are no longer looking at money through the lower window panes.

Of these four ways to make money having a job is the worst way to make money and owning a job is the second worst way to make money. I know that some of you self-employed job owners may be cringing at some of this information. Remember that having a job and owning a job have one major thing in common: your income is still limited by time, because you only have so much time. This means you can only make so much money.

The Best Way To Make Money

So, the two worst ways to make money are to have a job or own a job. Now we're going to look at money the way millionaires and billionaires make it. Let's look out the upper left-hand window pane, the O.A.S. window. O.A.S. stands for "Own A System". I like what Robert Allen and Mark Victor Hansen put together with the phrase they coined: "The word 'system' stands for Save-Yourself-Time-Energy and Money".

You want to own a system or, better yet, own some systems that pay you even when you're not working. There are different kinds of systems that you can own, but all of the systems that I'm talking about are what we call "business systems".

The Ebony Treasure Map

Most people don't have enough courage to start, create, and sustain a business system. You say, "Myron, what does it have to do with courage?" It actually has everything to do with courage. Here's why, while you're building a system, you're often not getting paid. You usually don't get paid until the system is built. But most of us are so "addicted" to a paycheck that we can't get rich. One of the biggest reasons we don't get rich is because we have to unlearn how to trade our time for money. You have to reprogram yourself for wealth creation instead of just "making ends meet" and "paying the bills". You've been programmed your whole life to trade your time for money: you have to put in eight hours work for eight hours pay.

First of all, what is eight hours pay? If I'm going to put in eight hours work, I'd like to put in eight hours work for a lifetime of residual income. Residual income is the kind of income that keeps coming in long after you stop going out to get it. If I'm going to put in 100 hours work, I'd rather put 100 hours work into something that's going to pay me for the rest of my life.

While you are creating a business system, you don't get paid. But after the system is created, it pays you from then on. You want to establish a business system because that is what's going to give you time and money freedom. This is where Bill Gates, Michael Dell, Sam Walton and the richest people in the world live. They own business systems.

This is the arena in which my millionaire friends and I play. We own systems that pay us five and six figures per month, even when we are not working. There are different kinds of business systems. There are people systems. There are business real estate systems. There are business technology systems. There are business license systems. There are many different kinds of systems that you can own.

When you are putting the system into place, you make little or no money, but after the system is in place, the money starts coming in so fast you can't even count it. So what you want to do is own a system or systems.

Establishing a system requires time. It requires effort. It requires energy. It requires money. It requires patience, because you don't generally start building a system one day and get paid the next. That's why most people don't do it. They think if they do some work that doesn't generate income right away, the effort wasn't worth it. I'm going to tell you something right now. Nothing could be further from the truth!

Building a business system is going to eventually give you time freedom and money freedom. It's going to give you more time at the end of your day, more time at the end of your week, more time at the end of your month, more time at the end of your year. It will give you more time to fulfill your life purpose. It won't be easy, but it will be worth it. I am glad that I learned a long time ago that success and failure are both hard. The difference is that if you succeed in life, you get to enjoy the fruits of your difficulty. If you fail in life, you have no fruit from your difficulty.

The Second Best Way To Make Money

The "S.M.S. window is the second best way to make money and the final way that we will discuss in this book, as we look through the Window of

Opportunity, S.M.S. means to Sow Money Seeds. This is investing in things like stocks, oil wells, gold mines, tax lien certificates, etc. This is where your money is making money for you. This is also where the richest people in the world live. This is where people like Warren Buffet hang out. These people understand how to make their money make money for them.

The beautiful thing about Sowing Money Seeds and planting your money is that, since everything reproduces after its own kind, when you begin to plant money, it makes your wealth grow at a faster and faster rate. You may be thinking money doesn't grow on trees, you're right, but if money did grow on trees, it would grow on money trees. Where else would money grow? Now I am speaking here figuratively. Money, if it is planted (invested), can grow more money.

You must learn to plant your money in your investments long enough for it to reproduce. Remember your money will never grow for you if all you do is use it for consumption. You must learn to use your money for production and reproduction.

CHAPTER FOUR

What Kind Of House Do You Live In?

Everyone lives in a house. Even homeless people live in a house. I'm not talking about the kind of house you are thinking of; I'm talking about your "Financial House". Just as there are different neighborhoods with different kinds of physical houses in them, there are different kinds of financial neighborhoods with different kinds of financial houses in them.

On the following pages, I am going to show you three different kinds of financial houses. I am going to show you the financial house of the poor. I am going to show you the financial house of the middle class. And then, I am going to show you the financial house of the rich. After you see these different kinds of financial houses, then you can decide which kind of house you desire and deserve to live in.

Now that you understand the four ways to make money, let's look at what people do with money after they get it. The biggest determining factor between the rich, poor, and middle class is not how much money they make; but what they do with money after they make it. To look at how we spend, save, invest and use our money, we are going to learn how to build a strong financial house. If your financial house is strong, then it will be able to weather any financial storm that comes along.

The Ebony Treasure Map

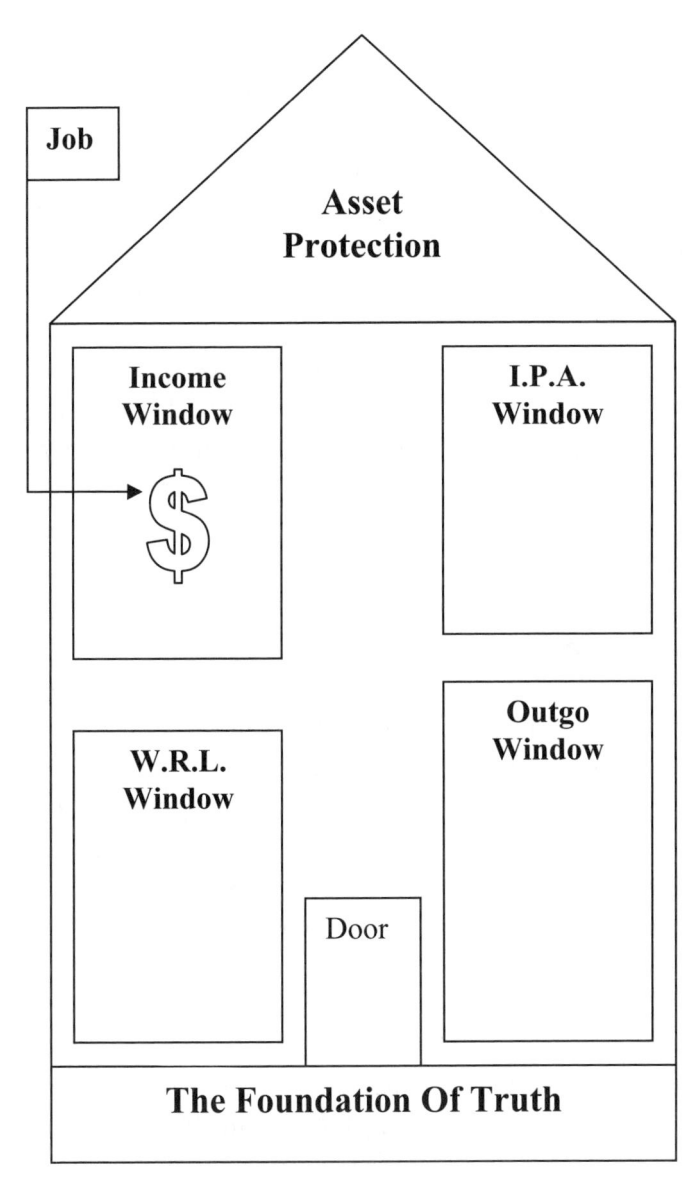

```
            Job
     Asset Protection
   Income Window        I.P.A. Window
         $
   W.R.L. Window        Outgo Window
              Door
     The Foundation Of Truth
```

Now let's look at the significance of this picture of a financial house. This principle has made me a fortune that is growing faster and faster, every month and every year. I want you to have the same experience, and you will, if you will allow yourself to accept, test, and follow the principles in this chapter.

Every house must be built on a foundation. This foundation is called, "The Foundation Of Truth". The roof on the house is called "Asset Protection". The upper left-hand window is the "Income Window". The bottom left-hand window is what I call the "WRL window", which stands for "Wealth Reducing Liabilities". The bottom right-hand window is called the "Outgo window". The upper right hand window is called the "IPA Window" or "Income Producing Asset Window". Together, all these components build a financial house.

Everyone lives in a financial house of some kind. There are three different kinds of financial houses to choose from. There is the financial house of the poor. There is the financial house of the middle class. Lastly there is the financial house of the rich.

People who live in the financial houses of the poor and the middle class don't realize that that is where they live. The poor and middle class think of their financial situation as "just the way things are".

Rich people are more aware of where they live financially, because they live there by decision. People who build a strong financial house; do so on purpose and they consistently and persistently build their houses with good financial principles, while the poor and middle class live their financial lives in a hap hazard manner hoping that everything will work out in the end. Let's look at the financial house of the poor.

The Ebony Treasure Map

The Financial House of the Poor

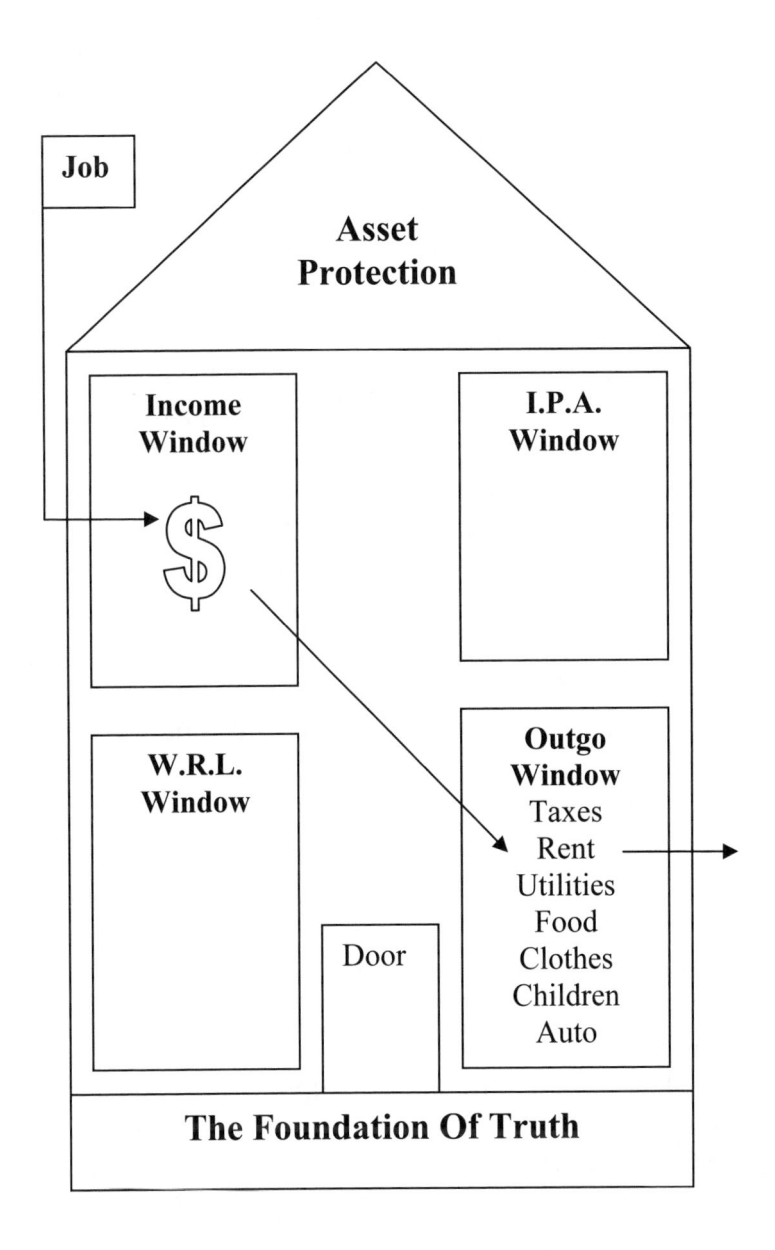

Job

Asset Protection

Income Window

$

I.P.A. Window

W.R.L. Window

Outgo Window
Taxes
Rent
Utilities
Food
Clothes
Children
Auto

Door

The Foundation Of Truth

Most people get their income (the money that comes into their financial house) from their job (also known as the journey of the broke). Whether you are rich, poor, or middle class is not determined by how much money you make at your job, but by what you do with your money after you make it.

We're going to see clearly here that rich people, poor people, and middle class people all do very different things with their money when they make it. Let's start out with people who are poor.

The reason that poor people are poor is not because they make a little bit of money, but because every dime that comes in the income window goes down and out the Outgo window.

The main reason that poor people are poor is because they believe that the only real purpose of money is spending it. If you spend your money, that means your money doesn't stay with you long enough to reproduce itself. It doesn't stay with you long enough to produce fruit. It doesn't stay with you long enough to have babies.

I like the term "pregnant money". You want money that has babies. When you have $100 bills, they have $100 babies. You want to make sure that when you have thousands of dollars, hold on to them long enough and invest them wisely enough so they have thousand-dollar babies. And when you have millions of dollars, they have million-dollar babies.

Do not be like poor people who spend every dime of every dollar. You must understand that the main purpose of money is not spending. The main purpose of money is reproducing more money. Don't spend the seed money; invest the seed money and then spend the fruit money. Art Williams (the founder of the A.L. Williams Corporation) wrote a little book called "Common Sense: A Simple Approach To Financial Independence". One of the principles that he revealed was that you should pay yourself first. Poor people pay themselves last, if they pay themselves at all.

Poor people spend all their money on taxes, rent, utilities, food, clothes, cable TV, etc. So, every dime that comes into a poor person's hand in the income window goes out of the Outgo window of their financial house.

For the average person, the biggest window in their house is the Outgo window. In fact, even the money they haven't made yet is already consumed by bills.

That's the motto of the poor. The motto of the poor is "I gotta pay the bills." Obviously, there is nothing wrong with paying your bills. It is something you definitely want to do, but if that's your main focus, you need to change it. Whatever you focus on expands.

So you don't want to focus on bills. You want to create such a great business system(s) that the bills are paid automatically and you don't even have to think about it.

Why is it that poor people focus on Outgo? Why is it that they focus on bills? I believe the emotional reason that they have this focus is because of fear: fear of losing their job, fear of not being able to feed their family and fear of not having what they need.

All this fear causes poor people to focus on how to "keep from not having" rather than focusing on what to do to have as much as they want. Fear causes poor people to stay poor. All of the money that comes into the income window comes down and goes out the Outgo window.

Taxes are the number one expense of poor people. Think about it: you're taxed when you earn your money; you're taxed when you spend it; you're taxed on what you own, now that you've bought it; you're taxed when you sell it; and, if you die, then they're really going to tax you.

Go back to page 32 and study the financial house of the poor. If you have any of the habits or tendencies of the poor, make sure that you break them and replace them with the principles that you are learning in this book. Remember the "Two Sentence Wealth Formula", the second sentence is: "Find out what poor people do financially and make sure you don't do it"!

Now let's take a look at the financial house of the middle class.

The Ebony Treasure Map

The Financial House of the Middle Class

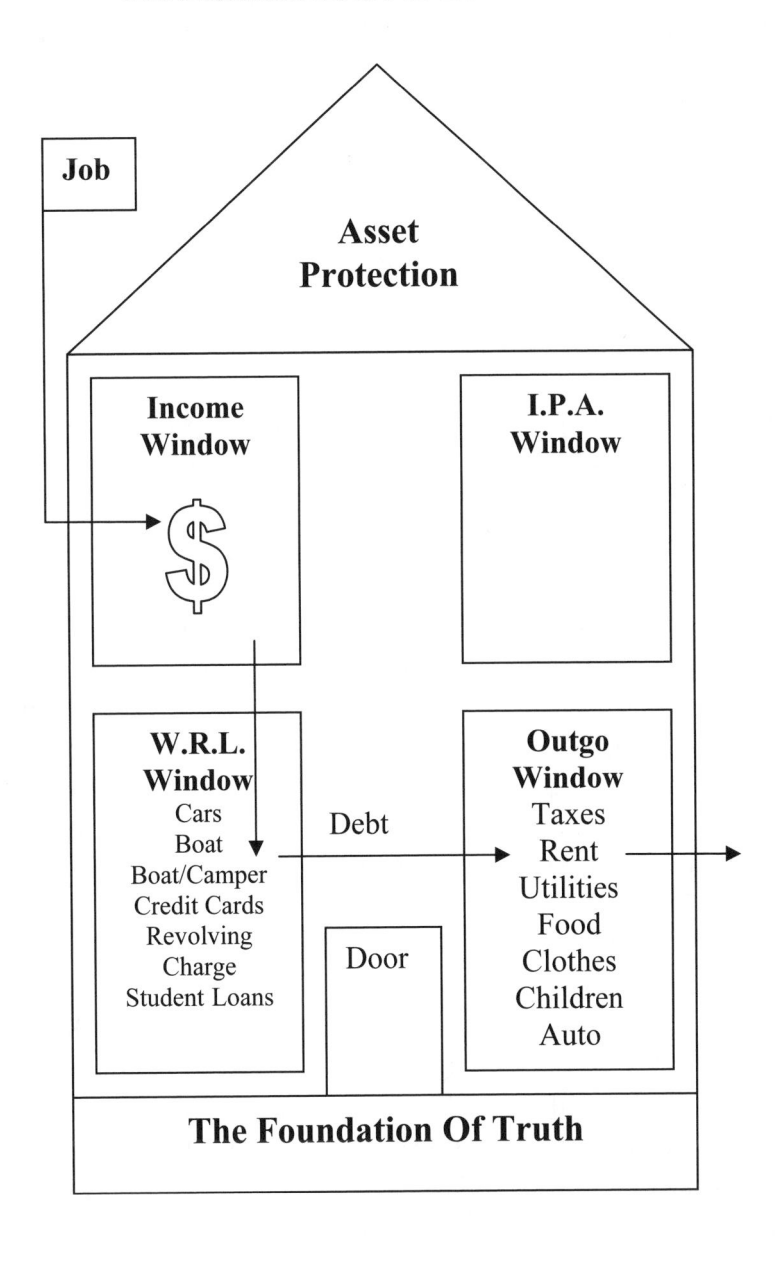

Job

Asset Protection

Income Window

$

I.P.A. Window

W.R.L. Window
Cars
Boat
Boat/Camper
Credit Cards
Revolving
Charge
Student Loans

Debt

Outgo Window
Taxes
Rent
Utilities
Food
Clothes
Children
Auto

Door

The Foundation Of Truth

The Ebony Treasure Map

Middle class people have a different focus. They take their money and they buy what I call "Wealth Reducing Liabilities". A wealth reducing liability is anything that you buy that takes money out of your financial house. The longer you own it, the more money it takes out of your financial house.

Here's how: If you buy these wealth reducing liabilities, or what I call "junk stuff", they only give you a temporary good feeling. Once the newness wears off, you're only left with a lot of expenses. You have to spend money to maintain this junk stuff and service the debt on it. This "feel good" expense continues to take money out of your financial house for years, if not decades.

Another problem with wealth reducing liabilities is that they don't hold their value in the marketplace. For example, you might spend $150 on a pair of jeans, but those jeans can't go back into the marketplace and sell for $150. So they don't have real value. You might spend $80,000-$90,000 on a car. There's nothing wrong with owning an $80,000 car, if you do it right. I own an $80,000 car. But what I'm saying is that if you spend your seed money to buy this stuff, then it's making you poorer, not richer.

I'm going to show you how you can get this stuff, the same $80,000 car, the same $500,000-$1,000,000 house, the same lifestyle that you're looking for, without taking money out of your income to do it.

The middle class motto is "I've got good credit," so they buy a new house. They don't pay rent. They get a mortgage and they get a house. But you can't park old cars in front of a new house, so they have to buy some new cars. Then the neighbor gets a boat, so they have to buy a boat. Then they have to get a truck to pull the boat, because you can't pull the boat with a car. Before you know it, they've bought all of this "junk stuff". They can't afford to pay cash for it, so they finance it, and they blow it out the "Outgo" window in the form of debt.

Middle class people focus on debt. Why? Middle class people focus on debt because they want to keep up with the Joneses. By wanting to keep up with the Joneses and have status, they end up spending more money than they make. They live their whole life in debt and then retire and become broke just like poor people. Remember the old saying, "If your outgo exceeds your income, then your upkeep will be your downfall."

If you truly desire to be rich, forget about having status. My definition of status is spending money that you don't have to buy something that you can't afford to impress somebody that you don't like, or worse, to impress people you don't even know.

I can remember one of the neighborhoods that I used to live in. There was so much "keeping up with the Joneses" going on there. One of my neighbors would buy a boat, then another neighbor would buy one; then another neighbor, and then another. It was one of the most amazing things that I have ever seen. One of my children said to me, "Dad, can we get a boat?" I said, "Yes son, we *can* get a boat, but we are not going to get a boat. We are going to use our money to create wealth, and not to create debt." He was pretty young then and could not understand why I wouldn't get a boat. I made up my mind a long time ago, that I wanted to be rich, more than I wanted to keep up with the Joneses. So while the Joneses were using their money to make them more broke, I was using my money to get richer. When you learn to use your money in this way, you will be amazed at how fast you can get rich. So gather your family around you and begin to teach them the principles in this book. One day, you will have a family legacy that you can be proud of, and your income will be growing like a wildfire.

Now before you go on to the next chapter; go back to page 37 and study the financial house of the middle class. Make sure you avoid thinking about money the way these people do.

So let's examine the financial house of the rich.

The Ebony Treasure Map

The Financial House of the Rich (In the beginning)

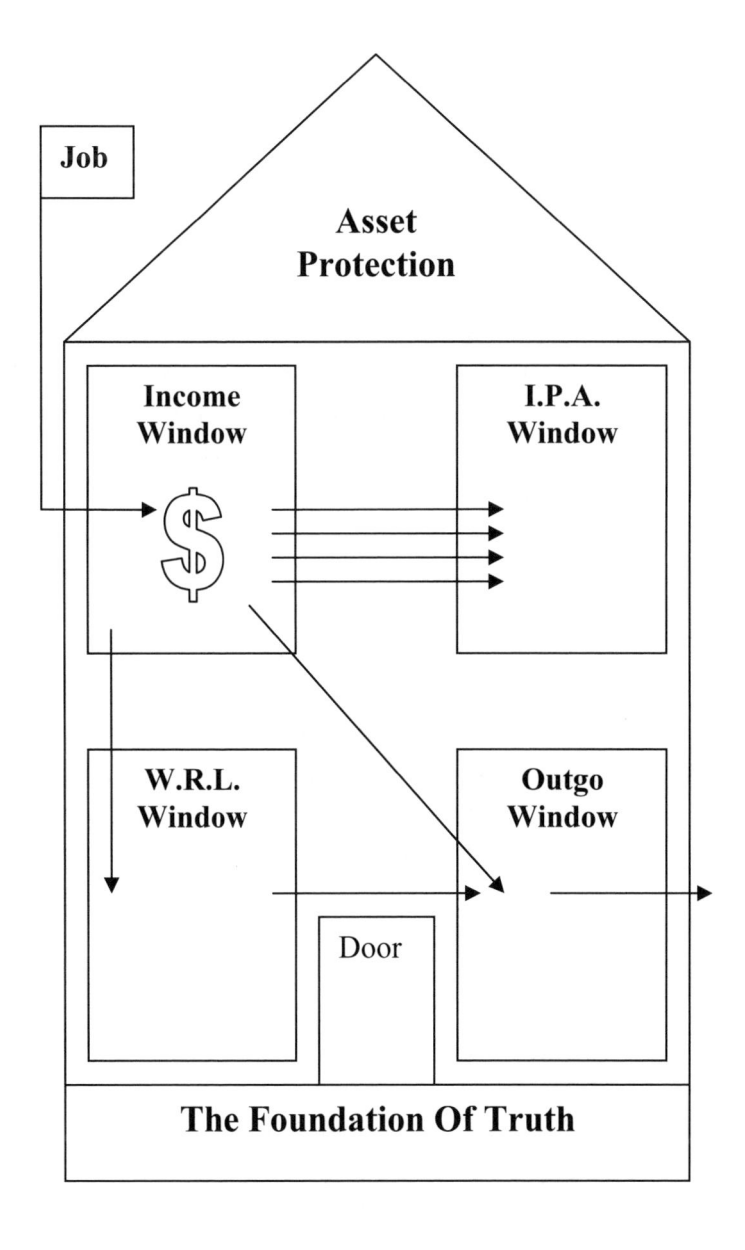

Job

Asset Protection

Income Window

I.P.A. Window

W.R.L. Window

Outgo Window

Door

The Foundation Of Truth

If you want real wealth, you're not going to be able to create it on the emotion of fear like poor people do, or on the emotion of envy like middle-class people.

What is the emotion that causes rich people to get rich? That's really a trick question. You don't get rich on emotion. If you're going to get rich, you're going to get rich on decision, not on emotion.

Income Producing Assets

Here's how that happens. You focus on the IPA window. The IPA window stands for "Income Producing Asset". An income producing asset is anything that brings money into your financial house, without you having to work for that money. You're not trading time for this money. You take some of your income in your early working days and put it over in your Income Producing Asset window. You start some kind of Income Producing Asset that can pay you when you're not working.

Most people can't think of any way to make money unless they are working for it. That is why most people are broke; because they don't know how to make money without working for it. Rich people know how to make money without working for it. I know they do, because they belong to the same country club that I belong to (or one like it). We're playing golf, while our employees are doing the work in our business. That business is called an asset.

Examples Of Income Producing Assets

An example of an Income Producing Asset could be real estate investments. If you own an apartment

The Ebony Treasure Map

building and it has 20 units in it and you rent those apartments out for $700 a piece, that apartment building brings in $14,000 a month. Let's say that the apartment building cost you $500,000. Your mortgage payment is $5,000 a month and your upkeep is $2,000 a month, so you are netting $7,000 a month on that real estate investment.

An Income Producing Asset could be a parking lot. A parking lot with a booth and one employee could be a very good income producing asset. The land for the parking lot can sometimes be bought very cheaply or even leased for a few years for free if you agree to clean up the lot after they tear down a building downtown or in a busy area, you pay to grade it, which may cost you $15,000. Even if you can't find a deal like this, you should be able to buy a lot for between $30,000 and $100,000. The booth might cost you $300 to put up. You pay someone $7-$8 an hour to run the booth and people pay you $5-$7 an hour to park there and that might bring in an extra $30,000-$40,000 a month.

Another Income Producing Asset might be a Laundromat, where people come and put coins in the washing machines and in the dryers. That might bring in $22,000 a month. Or you might own a car wash. That car wash generates $600,000 a year for you. These are Income Producing Assets that produce passive income for you without you actually being there.

You could also write a book. Every time the book sells, you get paid a royalty. Or you could write a song or produce an album and get royalties from that. Or you could come up with an idea or invention and license it to people or businesses. That license could make you wealthy.

The richest man in the world became wealthy through licensing. Bill Gates bought the DOS operating system back when the personal computer craze was launched. He bought it for $50,000 and, then, instead of selling it, he licensed it to IBM. Then he actually acquired the graphics user interface system from Apple (who acquired it from Xerox) and licensed it.

Bill Gates created this concept called Microsoft Windows. Every time somebody buys a PC for personal use, Bill Gates licenses that product to the buyer for approximately $299. That is a very powerful income producing asset.

The Microsoft Windows program has a CD in it that probably cost Bill Gates $.12 or less. It includes a book that probably cost Bill Gates $2.50, at the most, to produce. The box may be another $1. We'll say Bill Gates has $5 in materials invested in this software program, and he licenses the software to you. He doesn't sell it to you. He licenses it to you, so you can use it on a computer. That license costs you $299, even though it only cost him $5 to produce the actual product. That's what we call creating wealth. That is a business system.

Another Income Producing Asset could be a website. These are all things that take either money or time in order for you to produce.

Another great way for a person to get started enlarging their Income Producing Asset window is for a person to start a HBB, which is "Home-Based

The Ebony Treasure Map

Business"—Working from home through a concept called Network Marketing or multi-level marketing.

You may have a negative impression of Network Marketing because you may know of someone who had a bad experience in Network Marketing. Maybe they got started and maybe they worked hard for a couple of years and didn't make any real money. So you think that Network Marketing doesn't work.

Maybe you personally had a bad experience with Network Marketing. Maybe you got started with a Network Marketing company that made you a lot of promises and maybe the company went out of business, or other people around you were getting rich, but you weren't experiencing those kinds of results. If that's the case, don't worry.

What I want you to understand is that even if you get started in Network Marketing and you don't make a fortune, at least you started working on building an asset that pays you when you don't go to work.

I have income right now from a Network Marketing business that I built a long time ago that paid for both of my brand new cars: my 2006 Cadillac Escalade and my brand new 2006 Mercedes CLS 500 Coupe. My Network Marketing business also pays for my house. When I first got started in Network Marketing, I didn't know what I was doing. However, after I learned the skills of sales, leadership and empowerment, it didn't just make my Network Marketing Business better, it made my life better. Because of Network Marketing, I now have skills that I can use in any business venture I choose.

When faced with the lack of success I had with network marketing, most people would have quit. However, what I was doing back then (even though I didn't know I was doing it) was learning how to stop working for money. I was learning how to work to build an asset that would pay me from then on, even though it didn't pay me very much on the front end.

Network marketing does work. However, the reason many people don't make money when they begin Network Marketing is because they only know how to be employees. But in Network Marketing, they suddenly become business owners, but in reality, they are employees who own a business. They aren't business owners until they learn the skills of a business owner.

For us to think that Network Marketing doesn't work because either we've had a bad experience, or we know somebody who has, would be like saying that a person who has never driven a car before, never had a license, and never had a driving lesson should be able to start the car and get it out of the driveway. If they can't, it's the driver's fault; it's not the car's fault.

Maybe the driver does get the car out of the driveway and he drives down the road, gets ready to stop, but instead of stepping on the brake, he steps on the gas pedal. He runs through a red light or stop sign and has an accident. Again, we could say that cars are bad, but they aren't. It's the person's fault for not learning how to become the driver of the vehicle that they now own.

Let me say this: Network Marketing is a great vehicle, but until you learn how to drive it, it's not going to be a great vehicle for you.

Another good business you can put into your Income Producing Asset window would be to have a website or websites where you sell products. You can literally sell those products to people all over the world.

What happens when you first put time, money, effort, and energy into your Income Producing Asset window? When you first get started focusing on this window absolutely nothing happens. That's why most people will say, "This Income Producing Asset stuff, and being a business owner, doesn't work."

So what do they do? They go back to trading their time for money at their job and spending all the money they make. All the income goes out the Outgo window, or they buy junk stuff and blow it out the Outgo window in the form of debt.

Make a decision that you are going to focus on this "Income Producing Asset" window until it begins to produce massive amounts of cash for you. In the beginning, you will put a lot of time, a lot of effort, and a lot of energy into the "Income Producing Asset" window and nothing will happen. But, if you keep at it, eventually this Income Producing Asset will put some money back into your income window. Then it will put even more money back into your income window. Before you know it, you're putting a little bit of time, a little bit of effort, a little bit of income into your "Income Producing Asset" window, but it puts droves and droves of cash back into your income window.

Before long, your Income Producing Asset window will kick off so much cash that it will create your income for you. It will pay all of your bills. It will pay your house payment, your car payment, your utilities, your food, your clothes, plus it will buy all of your junk stuff—all of your computers and your PDAs and your Gameboys and your boats and jet skis and your motorcycle and your country club membership. It will pay for you to play at exotic golf courses all over the world.

Before you know it, your Income Producing Asset window will have gotten so big that it pays for everything in your financial house. Your Outgo Window and your Wealth Reducing Liability Window will have gotten so small that your Income Producing Asset window has almost consumed them. At this point your IPA window has become the biggest window in your house.

Now you've got a very, very strong financial house. Learn how to save some of that money in taxes through your roof which is called Asset Protection. You get to take advantage of a lot of the write-offs that rich people use and poor people never have the opportunity to take advantage of.

That's how you build a strong financial house. This concept changed my life forever. When I learned the concept of the four ways to make money with the Window of Opportunity and how to build a strong financial house, literally, my income went from $47,000 per year to $112,000 per year in just 12 months. Using the concept of the strong financial house, I've gone on to produce five-figure months, five-figure weeks, five-figure days. We've even gone on to produce some six-figure months and six-figure weeks. I have even had a six-figure day and a six-figure hour. On the next page you will see the financial house of the rich over time.

The Ebony Treasure Map

The Financial House Of The Rich (Over Time)

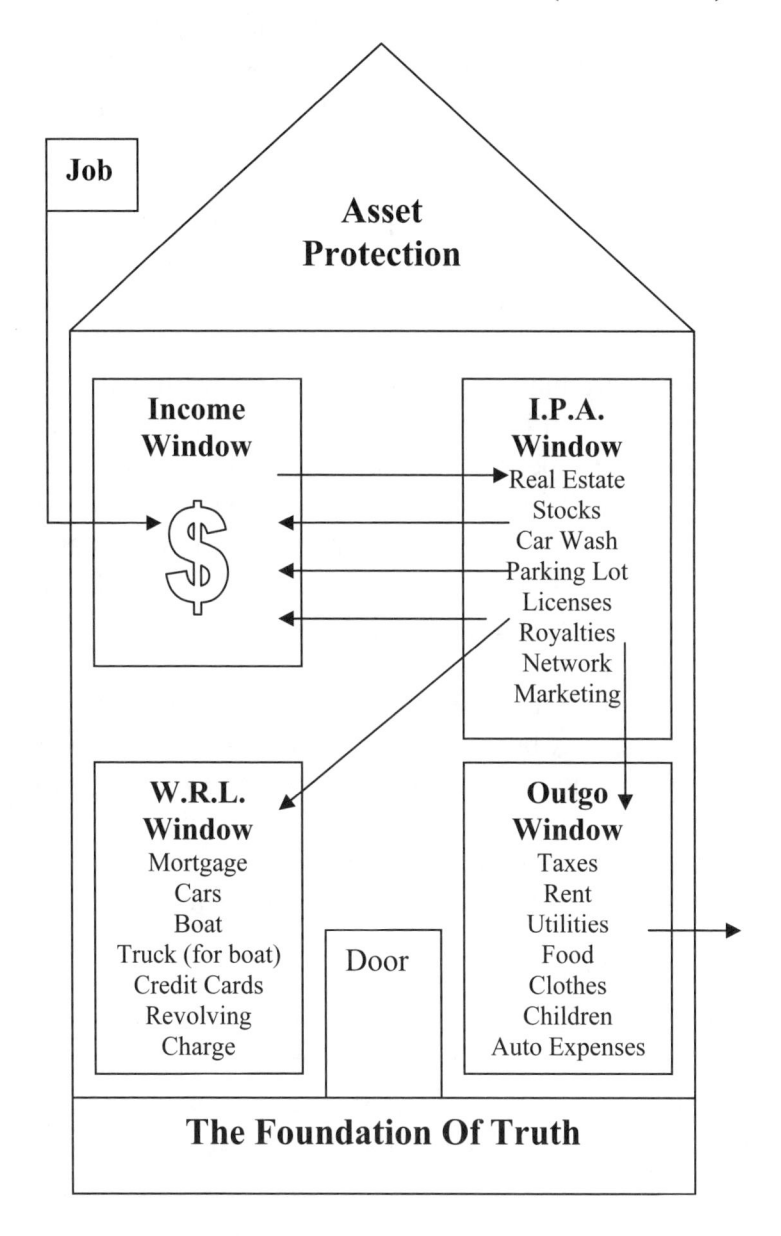

Job

Asset Protection

Income Window
$

I.P.A. Window
Real Estate
Stocks
Car Wash
Parking Lot
Licenses
Royalties
Network Marketing

W.R.L. Window
Mortgage
Cars
Boat
Truck (for boat)
Credit Cards
Revolving Charge

Door

Outgo Window
Taxes
Rent
Utilities
Food
Clothes
Children
Auto Expenses

The Foundation Of Truth

That is what can happen as you begin to build a strong financial house. Although all of the principles in this book can drastically impact your wealth, make sure you study this one about your financial house until you memorize it. Meditate on it, chew on it and focus on it until it is your natural way of thinking about money and what to do with it. I must warn you that this is going to be way outside the box of traditional thinking, or what I call "traditional non-thinking". I call it that because traditionally most people don't think. So understand this, if you are part of the small minority of people who do think you will be mocked, scoffed and even resented by some of the people closest to you for following this formula. Your friends and family will begin to whisper about you, they will think you are being unreasonable. But don't let that stop you. Remember don't take financial advice from people who are in the same place you are, or worse than you are.

It will be most difficult to follow these principles in the beginning, before the benefits show up. It will get easier with time, as your wealth begins to quietly grow and grow. So make a commitment to yourself from the very beginning to give these principles as much time as necessary to work in your life. I am looking forward to hearing your testimony on what has happened for you as your financial house and your financial neighborhood begin to change. It won't be long before your physical house and neighborhood will also change.

Let's go to the next chapter and look at how you can get all of these IPA businesses started.

CHAPTER FIVE

The Hands Free Money Business Plan

The Hands Free Money System business plan is very simple, but it's very powerful. I got the idea for it from a couple of Bible verses. In I Thessalonians 4:8-11 it says, "Study to be quiet and do your own business. Working with your hands is a thing that is good so that you might walk honestly towards them that are without and have lack of nothing."

Another verse is Ecclesiastes 5:3 and it says that "A dream cometh through a multitude of business". So I combined the essence of these two verses and came up with the Hands Free Money Business Plan. Here's how it works, since it said "work diligently with your hands" I knew that I dug enough ditches in my life and turned enough wrenches and hammered enough nails and sawed enough boards that I didn't want to use my hands in that capacity anymore. I decided I was going to use my hands for a concept. I was going to use my hands to create a business plan.

I decided that I wanted to start a business that I could run from my home and within two years have that business generating $10,000 a month in income. That $10,000 income had one requirement. After two years, it couldn't require any more than one finger's worth of effort in order to run it.

And when I got that business to $10,000 a month in income—then I'd start another totally different business that would generate another $10,000 a month for me within two years.

Then, two years later, I would start another business that would generate another $10,000 a month, so that six years down the road, I could be making $30,000 a month.

Then I decided that I would start another business and I would get it up to $10,000 a month in two years. But, all of these businesses would be businesses that were run from my home and wouldn't require more than a finger's worth of effort to run.

Then I started another business, and I created this business plan where I wanted to have, in twenty years, ten businesses paying me $10,000 a month and only requiring a finger's worth of effort from me to run.

The reason that it is so important that it only requires one finger's worth of effort to run is because I wanted to use my money to buy my time back. If I am making all of this money, but I am working like crazy, then I have defeated my purpose in starting a business in the first place.

Now let me define "one finger's worth of effort." One finger's worth of effort means that the work I do in that business can't interfere with my purpose in life or my passion in life. For instance, if I am an author, then whatever business I start must not take away from my time writing, after the business has been going for two years. If my passion is playing golf (and it is), then after two years that business shouldn't interfere with me playing golf several times per week or even every day, if I choose. The last thing about the one finger's worth of effort is this: the business must free up enough of my time that it allows me to start another business. Now where do you start?

I started out with a concept called Network Marketing. That was my first business model. Then I started a business selling things on the Internet. Then I started my training company where I get to travel and see exotic places in the world.

Then I started another business, which is my Ebay business. Then I started another business, my record label, which is my music business. Then I started another business where I sell merchant accounts to people all over the country who want to be able to process credit cards for their businesses. Then I also started an investment business where I invest my money and manage my own money.

Then I started a coaching and consulting practice. Then I started my teleseminar business.

These nine businesses can make anywhere from an extra $1,400 a month to $100,000 plus a month per business per business. You combine them all and they create a very, very powerful income.

The beautiful thing about this business plan is that it's so simple that a fifth grader can understand it and anybody can do it. If you're not comfortable with setting an income goal of $10,000 per business, pick a number you are comfortable with. Maybe it's $5,000 per month per business, or 3 businesses at $2,000 a month. Once you achieve your goals, raise the numbers.

CHAPTER SIX

All Businesses Are Not Created Equal

Now that you have a business plan, you need to start the right kind of business. You want to make sure you start a business that is not a job. You want to start a business that is a system. The best way I know to do this is to start a product-oriented business instead of a service-oriented business.

The reason this is so important is because providing a service requires your time; which limits the amount of money you are able to make in that business. If you start a business that sells a product, you are not limited by time. You can sell one product or 100,000 products in the same exact amount of time. Therefore, there is no limit on your income. Makes sense, right? However, this understanding creates two more very important questions. What products should you sell, and how should you sell them? You have far too many choices of products and ways to sell them for me to cover them all in this book. For starters, you can sell information products, health products, entertainment products, electronic products, software products and business products, to name a few.

How do you sell them? You can sell them as a Manufacturer's Rep, in a catalog, on the Internet, in a magazine through classified ads, on eBay or through an affiliate program. You can also sell products through a Network Marketing company. While Network Marketing is not for everyone, it certainly is a business model that works very well for those who are willing to learn it. Only you know if that is where you should start. But in my opinion, it is well worth investigating.

While I don't believe that everyone should start with Network Marketing, I do recommend it for most people for several reasons.

Ten Good Reasons To Do Network Marketing

1. **When you start out in Network Marketing, you don't need talent.** I have found in all of my years of Network Marketing, that you only need two skills in the beginning. These two skills will help you aquire all of the other necessary skills. So here they are again, you must be coachable and you must be available.

2. **When you start out in Network Marketing, you have the opportunity to learn new and valuable skills.** These new skills will be worth more to you than the money that you make in Network Marketing. They include networking, selling, recruiting, leadership development, public speaking, and creating and promoting events. You'll learn how to get people to do what you want them to do for their own reasons and benefit. These skills will help every one of your other businesses become successful so much faster, because you'll have a good skill set. Don't worry, you don't have to start out with these skills and there will be other successful people who will have a vested interest in your learning these skills and they will coach you free of charge.

3. **You have an above-average chance of becoming rich.** Some of the richest people in any community are people who got rich through Network Marketing. I know people who make six figures a month. You may not make that much in Network Marketing, but at least you would have an equal opportunity. Think how your life would change, if you made an extra $3,000-$5,000 a month in Network Marketing. It would also give you some passive income to invest, and free up some extra time.

4. **Network Marketing pays you for results.** It doesn't just pay you for time. If you go out and produce stellar results in Network Marketing, that business will pay you a stellar paycheck.

5. **You get to multiply or leverage your time in Network Marketing.** If you work five hours a week and you get two other people to work five hours a week, you're getting paid for 15 hours of work but you're only doing five. If those two people go get two more people apiece and they each do five hours of work, that's 20 more hours. You're getting paid for 35 hours of work, even though you are only doing five.

When you get to the place in your Network Marketing career where you actually have thousands of people out working every week, generating a paycheck for themselves and a paycheck for you, you have leveraged yourself in an incredible way.

6. **When you get started in Network Marketing, you get surrounded by positive people.** I

can't say enough about surrounding yourself with positive, upbeat, excited people. That alone will charge your emotional battery and make you want to work.

7. Network Marketing has an unlimited upside. There is no cap on your income potential. Network Marketing can give you money freedom and time freedom.

8. You get to travel to some of the greatest places in the world. A lot of Network Marketing companies have contests that allow you the opportunity to win free trips and go to some of the most exotic places in the world, and the company pays for it. (Now that's a real paid vacation).

9. Let's not forget the bonuses. A lot of Network Marketing companies have what they call "Car Bonus Programs" where they will actually pay for a brand new car for you to drive if you produce "x-amount" of dollars of volume. That's an exciting program. You will learn to become successful while the company pays for you to drive a brand new car.

10. The business is willable and transferable. Your family gets to keep that income that you've created, for generations. You can actually create a legacy for your family.

CHAPTER SEVEN

Leverage Your Business through Technology

Now that you have a business plan and you've started a product-based business, make sure that you leverage your business through technology. One of the biggest challenges that we black people have in starting a business is that we don't use technology. We become techno phobic instead of techno friendly.

Learn to use technology. Learn to use fax machines, email and the Internet. These different technologies give you leverage that can catapult your business or businesses and help you earn an extremely large amount of money in a very, very short period of time.

When you use the Internet, you are tapping into a technology where you have access to hundreds of millions of people at the same time. If you can tap into the right market, you have the ability to become a multi-multi-millionaire, faster than any other way I know.

If you have picked the right market, the right product and the right sales process online, you have literally struck gold. Then, when a buzz begins and people start talking about your product and your website, your website can, literally, go very, very high in Internet rankings in a very short period of time. But more importantly, the sales can start to pour in so fast, it will make your head spin. You can then start capitalizing on that through technology.

There are several things that you want to do when you start to use the technology of the Internet to leverage your business.

Build Email Lists

First, you want to build an email list. On the Internet, the email address and the first name is gold, so build a huge email list. This will give you a database of people to send your marketing messages to.

Every time you create, buy, or acquire the rights to a new product, it gives you a whole new wave of sales with your existing customer base. You want to build a list of names and email addresses. Make a commitment to yourself right now that from this day forward, every time you meet somebody, you will get their name and their email address, and ask them if it would be ok to maintain contact with them via email. When you are doing that, you are opening up a whole new world of profits and leveraging yourself through technology.

Become A Savvy Internet Marketer

You definitely want to become an Internet Marketer. There are many different sites on the Internet, but in this book we will only discuss 3 types.

1. **The "Brochure Site".** This type of site is the most popular kind of website online. (It is also one of the least profitable). A brochure site basically gives your customer a bunch of nebulous information about you or your company. The reason I say that this type of site is the least profitable is because your customer doesn't come to your site for you. Your customer comes to your site because they see your site as a solution to their

problem. If your site is not a solution to their problem or if the solution is too hard to find, they will leave and go looking elsewhere.

    2. **The "Capture Site"** is also known as a squeeze page. The sole purpose of this "site" or more accurately stated "page" is to capture the name and email of your potential customer before you even let them see your site. Once they give you what you want (their name and email address), then you let them in to find the solution to their problem. If you want to see a capture page, you can go to www.conferencecallfortunes.com .

    3. **The "Sales Site"** (A.K.A. a sales setter site) can rake in cash like crazy. If you have done a good job picking your market and developing your message, then your website sales will start to pour in so fast it will scare you. This is especially true if your product actually works. If you want to see an example, check out www.biggerbetterfastermlm.com. This was the very first site that I built. If you want to see a few more examples of sales letter sites, here are a couple of my favorites.

www.speedysponsor.com
www.successoperatingsystem.com.
www.moreheartmasters.com
www.inpowermentrecords.com

    Yes, it's good to have brochure websites like most people have, but make sure a brochure website points to different "sales sites" for individual products that you sell. That way, somebody can come to that page and discover the product that you sell, how much you sell it for, and all the reasons why they should buy it. That's what happens when you tap into the power of technology.

I started selling on the Internet with "Sales Sites" 13 months ago. I was hoping that I would make $400-$500 my first month because I had already been in business for several years. I already had a "webmaster" build me a website. I paid thousands of dollars for that site, but that site did not generate me $100 in profits in the two years, that's when I decided to take matters into my own hands. I will show you my monthly sales from my websites since I started to market my products on the Internet 13 months ago.

Before I show you my results, I want to give you a disclaimer, because I don't want you to get the wrong idea about making money with technology. I just want you to know what is possible.

Disclaimer:

Earning and Income statements made by our company are estimates of what we believe you can possibly earn. There is no guarantee that you will make these levels of income, and you accept the risk that the earnings and income statements differ by individuals.

As with any business, your results will vary, and will be based on your individual capacity, business experience, expertise, and level of desire. There are no guarantees concerning the level of success you may experience. The testimonials and examples used are exceptional results, and are not intended to represent or guarantee that anyone will achieve the same or similar results. Each individual's success depends on his or her background, dedication, desire and motivation.

The Ebony Treasure Map

There is no assurance that examples of past earnings can be duplicated in the future. We cannot guarantee your future results and/or success. There are some unknown risks in business and on the Internet that we cannot foresee which can reduce results. We are not responsible for your results.

The Numbers

Now that we took care of the disclaimer, here is what my numbers have been over the last thirteen months and for the first eight days of my fourteenth month.

Month	Orders Count	Gross Sales	Net Sales
June 2005	65	$6324.00	$5862.00
July 2005	56	$5163.80	$4895.00
August 2005	76	$6724.20	$6471.50
September 2005	65	$5229.80	$4922.50
October 2005	47	$5602.50	$5350.50
November 2005	48	$6678.50	$6377.50
December 2005	92	$10248.00	$9686.50
January 2006	45	$3720.11	$3495.41
February 2006	56	$4766.50	$4450.00
March 2006	98	$7822.84	$7359.44
April 2006	115	$8496.50	$8090.50
May 2006	78	$7875.82	$7614.12
June 2006	95	$7892.35	$7507.75
July 2006	119	$16665.70	$15896.00
August 2006	25	$2036.00	$1924.00
Grand Total	**1080**	**$105246.62**	**$99902.72**

This illustration was taken directly off of my website shopping cart and is the month-to-month sales since I started selling online in June of 2005. Making money on the Internet was challenging to learn, but once I acquired some skills, it took off like a rocket. I don't even use all of the tools that I could use, because I am having too much fun playing golf every day.

One Of The Best Ways To Learn How To Sell Online

I have found that one of the best ways to learn to sell online is to start using eBay. If you start buying and selling on eBay, it will give you a good idea of how the Internet Marketing strategies work. It is also a great place to do market research. You can find out what products are hot on eBay by doing a search and seeing what items have lots of bids beside them. I see eBay as microcosm of the Internet as a whole. If something is hot on eBay, it will be even hotter on a sales letter site. By the way, when you sell something on eBay, long sales letters work there as well. Not only is eBay a huge marketplace, but it is a growing marketplace. The last time I checked, there were over 600,000 people, in the U.S. alone, who consider selling on eBay to be their full-time job.

You can tap into the power of technology. You just need to discover a niche and discover where those people are searching online. Where are they hanging out online? What are they researching online? Provide that information for them. If you are a person who does a good job of bringing information to your niche, then you can make a fortune on the Internet. You want to leverage your time with technology.

Tap Into Teleseminars

Another method of using technology to leverage your income is by doing teleseminars and conference calls. I have made between a few hundred dollars to $12,000 in a single hour by doing seminars on the telephone. I send people an email that invites them to participate in a teleseminar. Sometimes the seminars are free and sometimes there is a registration fee. When people come to the teleseminar, I teach them something. I then give them an opportunity to buy a product to assist them with what they've learned. I use the teleseminar to drive traffic to my website where I sell them a product. It's absolutely incredible. If you want to learn more about how to make really big money doing teleseminars and conference calls, visit my website at www.conferencecallfortunes.com and register with your name and email address. When you go to that website, you'll have the opportunity to get a free conference call bridge line.

When I first starting doing teleseminars and conference calls: my conference bridge cost me $75 a month. But I am going to give you a free conference call bridge through "Golden Teleconferencing". So go to www.conferencecallfortunes.com, register for free, and then the second page will tell you how to get your own free conference bridge.

You'll also see I have a CD program that you can purchase called "Conference Call Fortunes". Pick up some of those resources so you can learn to leverage your time and your income through teleseminars.

I like what Archimedes said. "If you give me a lever long enough and a prop strong enough, I can single-handedly move the world." I believe that there have never been levers as long as the ones we have now with the Internet. There have never been props as strong as the Internet and teleconference bridges. There are people who literally make over a million dollars in a single month utilizing these technologies.

I want you to capitalize on it and tap into it. The more you tap into it and the more other people tap into it, the more there is for everyone. So tap into the power of technology.

CHAPTER EIGHT

It's Better To Be A V.M. Than It Is To Be A V.P.

You may have never heard of a VM, but I know you know what a VP is: A V.P. is a Vice President. People love that title. They want to be the Vice President of this and the Vice President of that. They want to be the Senior Vice President, The junior Vice President, the regional Vice President and the Vice President's Vice President.

But you would be much better off as a V.M. What is a VM? A V.M. is a Virtual Millionaire. A virtual millionaire is a person who does not have a million dollars accumulated, but has a million-dollar lifestyle.

There Are Different Types Of Millionaires

There are also asset millionaires, cash millionaires, and virtual millionaires. (A virtual millionaire is a different kind of asset millionaire). Many people don't realize that many virtual millionaires are much better off than traditional asset millionaires, because many asset millionaires don't have enough cash flow. Virtual millionaires have cash flow and lots of it. Let me explain.

A liquid millionaire or a cash millionaire is a person who has a million dollars in cash. That means that they could write a check for a million dollars and the check would clear.

The second kind of millionaire is an asset millionaire. In other words, they own a million dollars or more of equity. According to Paul Zane Pilzer, one of the nation's foremost financial economists and financial forecasters, over the next ten years, ten million new millionaires will be created and developed in this country alone. That's right, ten million new millionaires in the next ten years. My question to you is, "Will you be one of them?"

An asset millionaire is the kind of millionaire he's speaking of. That's a person who has over a million dollars in net worth. That means that if you own two million dollars in real estate and you have one million dollars in equity you don't owe money for, then you are an asset millionaire; you own a million dollars in assets. You could also explain it like this: if you add up all of your liabilities and subtract them from the total of all of your assets, if the difference is over a million dollars, you are an asset millionaire.

Let's talk about a virtual millionaire. A virtual millionaire is my favorite because it's one of the easiest ways to become a millionaire. You can become a virtual millionaire in less than twelve months. Before I explain what a virtual millionaire is, let me ask you this. Working like you are working right now, making the amount of money that you're making, doing what you do for a living, how long would it take you to become a liquid millionaire if you saved 100% of your income?

Let me help you understand exactly how long it would take. If you make $25,000 a year and you save every dime of it and don't pay taxes on it (which I don't recommend), it would take you 40 years to become a cash millionaire, if you save all of your money at 0% interest.

I don't know about you, but I don't know anybody who is saving 100% of what they make. Let's say you've got to make at least $50,000 to save $25,000 a year. So if you make $50,000 a year and you save half of it, then 40 years from now you could be a cash millionaire.

Let's say that you make $100,000 a year and you save half of that, or $50,000. It would take you 20 years to become a cash millionaire. Don't forget to calculate taxes into the equation. When you start making $100,000 a year, you will be taxed in the 30% to 50% tax bracket.

Let's say that you are in a 30% tax bracket. That means that you have $70,000 net money coming in. You're saving $50,000 which means you are living off of $20,000 a year. It would still take you 20 years to become a cash millionaire. You can see why most people never become a cash millionaire. Most people never become a liquid millionaire.

If you're going to become an asset millionaire, it doesn't take nearly as long, especially if you have good credit. You can go out and buy some real estate properties and, over time, accumulate some equity because of appreciation and because of paying down the mortgages. You can accumulate some pretty good equity over time. Let's say you could become an asset millionaire in ten years through real estate or some other kind of investment. Everybody would agree that's good. But, that doesn't necessarily give you cash flow.

Cash flow is king. Positive cash flow is really what you want. You want your money coming in faster than it's going out. In fact, you want to be in supersonic positive cash flow. You want to be in hyper-speed positive cash flow. You want to be in turbocharged positive cash flow. You want the money coming in two times, three times, four times, even ten times faster than you're spending it.

There's not a person reading this book right now who would disagree with that statement. You want your money coming in a whole lot faster than it's going out. You may be wondering, "How do you accomplish this?" That's a great question.

You do it by becoming what I call a "virtual millionaire". Here's why I call it that. If you had a million dollars invested at 6%: the million dollars would give you $60,000 a year in cash flow, without ever touching the million dollars. (Six percent of a million is $60,000.) If you divide that $60,000 into twelve months, that would give you $5,000 a month. So if you had a million dollars invested at 6% you could live off that interest. It would pay you $60,000 a year. Even though you're a millionaire, your millionaire lifestyle means you don't have to work and you net about $60,000 a year. That's a million dollar a year lifestyle.

What I call a virtual millionaire is someone who builds a business that produces for them at least $5,000 a month that they don't work for. When you've got a business that generates $5,000 a month in passive income, that's when you are what I call a VM—a virtual millionaire—and you are living the "virtual millionaire reality".

Let me ask you this. Which would take you longer to do? Save a million dollars so you could live off of 6%, or develop a business that pays you $5,000 a month? As soon as you spent one dollar, you would no longer be a millionaire. However, if you invested it and you got the $60,000, you would still be a millionaire. You could still have a lifestyle where you didn't have to work for money.

Your question right now is probably, "What kind of business could you start that you don't have to work that could pay you $5,000 a month?" Actually, all of the businesses I mentioned earlier could generate that kind of income. You could start a Network Marketing business. You could start an Internet Marketing business. You could do Real Estate. You could buy a parking lot. You could buy a Laundromat or vending machines or a car wash. Any kind of business that does not require your presence in order for you to get paid is the kind you want to start. Then you can be a virtual millionaire. I don't want you to think that I am saying that becoming a V.M. doesn't require any work, because it does require work to get there. However, once you have gotten there that is when the income comes in with out you going out to get it.

I want you to have a goal, a dream and a desire to live the virtual millionaire reality (on your way to becoming a liquid millionaire). You know what's better than being a virtual millionaire? Being a virtual multi-millionaire is better than being a virtual millionaire. If you can build a business that generates $10,000 a month without you going to work, you have literally built a business that is worth $2,000,000.

If you can generate $15,000 a month in passive income that you don't have to go out and directly earn, then you have just built a business that is worth $3,000,000. I think you get the picture.

If you've got a business that you don't have to touch for a month, two months, three months, five months, six months, a year, two years—yet month after month it pays you $15,000 a month—you literally have a business that is worth $3,000,000. It's the exact same thing as having $3,000,000 invested at 6%.

On the next page let's look at what your financial house would look like in this situation.

The Ebony Treasure Map

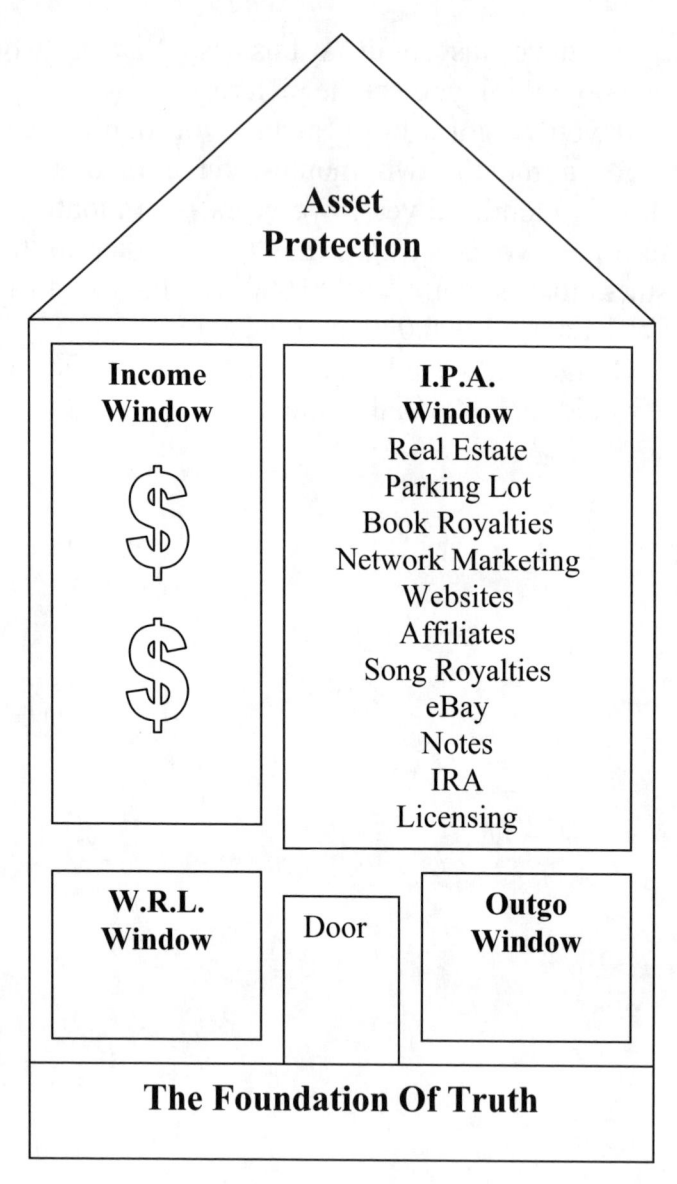

```
                    /\
                   /  \
                  /    \
                 /      \
                /  Asset \
               / Protection\
              /_____\
              |            |
              | Income  | I.P.A.    |
              | Window  | Window    |
              |         | Real Estate
              |   $     | Parking Lot
              |         | Book Royalties
              |         | Network Marketing
              |   $     | Websites
              |         | Affiliates
              |         | Song Royalties
              |         | eBay
              |         | Notes
              |         | IRA
              |         | Licensing
              |_____|_____|
              | W.R.L. |Door| Outgo |
              | Window |    | Window|
              |_____|____|_____|
              | The Foundation Of Truth |
              |_____|
```

You can see in this illustration that your IPA window is the biggest window in your financial house. Your income window is the second biggest window.

The Ebony Treasure Map

When you get to this point, your outgo window and WRL window are so small you almost don't even notice them anymore.

That is such a cool concept, because that is how you can live like a millionaire on your way to becoming one. That's the virtual millionaire reality. You want to become a VM instead of focusing on becoming a V.P.

CHAPTER NINE

Know What Business You're Really In

Most business owners have no idea what business they are in. People who start a plumbing business think they are in the business of plumbing. People who start a hotel think they are in the business of hotels. People who write books think they are in the business of writing books. People who make movies think they are in the business of making movies. While this thinking seems logical, nothing could be further from the truth.

If you own a business, yet you don't know what business you are in, you won't be in business very long. While you are in it, it will be a very long, arduous, and difficult process. The real business you are in and every other business owner is in; is the business of marketing.

A lot of authors are starving because they don't understand that they're not in the writing business. They write books, but they are really in the book marketing business. If you write a book and you don't know how to market your book, you're going to be broke.

There are people, who have written many, many, many great books, but they didn't know how to market them and now they're broke. There are great musicians who don't know how to do marketing and they're broke. There are great actors and actresses, that don't know how to do marketing and they're broke. There are people who are involved in all kinds of businesses, but are broke, because they don't know how to do marketing. But, the people who are average at their business, but great at marketing, make a fortune.

The difference between rich business owners and broke business owners is marketing. The most important thing is not how good the movie is, because all of us have seen a bad movie. The most important thing is not how good the song is, because we've all heard crappy songs by crappy singers with crappy music. The most important thing is not how good the book is. What matters most is "How good are you at selling and marketing it?"

People who are good at selling something bad make more money than people who are bad at selling something good. I'm not recommending that you sell something that is bad. I want you to sell great products that give great value. But if you create them and you can't sell them, it doesn't really matter that you created them. The only person it matters to is you.

When you understand that marketing is the business you are in, then you will understand that your business never starts with you. It never starts with your invention. Your idea should never start with your idea. It never starts with your book. Your song should never start with your song. Your movie should never start with your movie. Your business should always start with the marketplace. What do people want? That is the most important question in business. Because the marketplace is never wrong.

In marketing, the main question is, "What do the people want?" If you've got a large enough group of people who are hungry for something, and you are good at letting them know you have it, you can become a multi-millionaire very quickly. That is why you've got to learn how to do these two things. You've got to go out and learn how to find the hungry people. And you've got to learn how to tell them that you've got what they are hungry for. Then you will be in the business of marketing.

The Best Definition of Marketing I've Ever Heard

The following sentence is the best definition of marketing I've ever heard. *Marketing is the art and science of discovering and developing in other people* (that's really important—in other people) *the desire for more and more of your product, service or opportunity.* THAT is marketing. The reason I say it is the best definition of marketing I've ever heard is because I couldn't find a definition of marketing that I liked, so I made that one up.

Marketing is not handing out brochures. Marketing is not handing out business cards. Marketing is not handing out information. That's not marketing. Marketing is the art and science of discovering and developing in other people a desire for more and more of your product, service, or opportunity.

Marketing is what you must become an expert at, if you want to become wealthy. It doesn't matter how good of a writer you are. It doesn't matter how good of a singer you are if you are horrible at marketing. The thing that matters most is "How good are you at marketing?" That's the thing that you want to become an expert in. You will make your fortune when you become an expert in marketing.

Let me give you an example. When you go to any of my websites—
www.conferencecallfortunes.com,
www.successoperatingsystem.com,
www.biggerbetterfastermlm.com,
www.ebonytreasuremap.com,
www.successjams.com, etc.
—you will find an example of great marketing.

Why? Because I give you something for free and you give me your name and email address. If you like what I gave you for free, when I come up with something that I'm not giving away for free, but I'm selling it for $7, $17, or $27 or $37, or $47, or $57, $67, $77, $87, $97 or $197 or $397, some of you will buy some of those things. That's called marketing. I give you something of value for free and you come back for the products I sell.

If you perceive the value in the free item, then you will take me up on my offer when I have something that you can buy from me. Why? Because you feel that if I gave you something of value for free, then the thing I want to sell must really be good.

That's called marketing. I want you, as a business owner, to become an expert in marketing. When you do, your entire life will change. When you come to the Six Figure Business School, you are going to learn so many incredible marketing techniques that it will absolutely knock your socks off.

Understand what business you are really in. You are in the business of marketing your business. If you own more than one business, you are in the business of marketing your businesses.

CHAPTER TEN

Find A Treasure Guide Who Has Already Found The Treasure

In the arena of money I have found an amazing phenomenon: People who are broke will not take financial advice from people who are rich, but they will take financial advice from people who are broke.

One of the greatest keys to becoming successful in your financial life in general is to find a treasure guide who has already found the treasure. If you want to become a millionaire, if you want to live the life of the rich and famous, you have to make sure that you find a treasure guide who has already found the treasure.

This is critical because these guides know how to take you to where the treasure is. They can also show you some great ways to get the treasure that you wouldn't have figured out in a lifetime. So find somebody who has found the way and follow them. If they ask you to do something or give you some advice that doesn't make sense to you, ask them to clarify; if you still don't understand do it anyhow! After it works you will understand more clearly, because you will have a brand new perspective. I'm not suggesting that you follow people blindly. But, if what your mentors and teachers are saying to you doesn't make sense; it could be because they are looking at the subject of making money from a totally different perspective. That perspective usually won't make sense to you until you learn to look at things from the same side of money they do. When you don't understand what your mentors and teachers are showing you, just trust it until you can see it.

Find somebody who has found the treasure and get them to take you by the hand and lead you into the financial Promised Land.

Don't listen to your broke friends anymore, you know, the ones that try to convince you that everything is a scam. Stop listening to your broke friends who have never tried anything, or never made any real money and still work for "the man." If you don't want to have a job for the rest of your life, don't take financial advice from people who have a job.

Every so often I'll have somebody from an investment firm call me. Usually they have young employees who are trying to sell me some investments. I'll ask them two questions that invariably get them a little ticked off, because they want one thing and I want something else.

The first question I ask is, "Do you own this investment?" Most of the time they say "no", the second question I ask them is, "Are you a millionaire?" They say, "Well, what difference does it make?" "Well, the difference it makes is this. I'm asking you the question, 'Are you a millionaire'?" "No, I'm not." Then I make this recommendation to them, "I want you to go invest in the same investment you are recommending to me. Then come back to sell it to me after it works for you, because I don't take financial advice from people who are not millionaires." I know that someone who has a job selling investments, and is making $50,000-$60,000 a year, hasn't found the Treasure Map yet.

The Ebony Treasure Map

I have figured out the Treasure Map. I have not had a regular job for twelve years. Therefore, when I get financial advice, I get it from people who are making a whole lot more money than me. (I will soon have to start getting advice from billionaires). I don't take financial advice from people who are struggling, people who are broke, people who are making less money than me, or people who are making the same amount of money that I make.

I may occasionally get ideas from people who make the same amount I do, but I don't take financial advice from them. I like people who have been there, done that, got ten t-shirts to take me by the hand and lead me by the hand so that I can get my t-shirts.

Find a guide who has already found the treasure and get them to take you by the hand and lead you where they found it. That is one of the most important things that you will ever do on your financial journey.

CHAPTER ELEVEN

You Have No Competition

The next thing you want to do is understand that you have no competition. Most people allow the fact that there is competition to cause them to be afraid to even try.

I was speaking this past year at my children's school in their entrepreneurial class. One of the questions a student asked me was, "Mr. Golden, what do you do about competition?" My answer shocked this young lady. I told her, "There is no competition." I have no competition in business whatsoever.

In fact, I have friends who are in the same business that I am and I recommend their products and promote them and their products to the people who are in my database, because I am not worried about someone stealing my customers. Why? I have no competition.

The reason I have no competition is because I don't base my financial model on the current philosophy of economics. This model basically states that competition is basically good because it make business better, because it causes people to excel in business. While I do believe that we ought to seek to excel in business, I don't believe that there is any competition.

Here's what I mean. Most people believe in an "economic pie". You've heard people talk about getting their piece of the pie. Some people don't want to become wealthy because they have bought into this philosophy. They believe that the economy is like a pie and the more they get, the less there is for anybody else. Or the more that those mean, bad, rich people get, the less there is for the rest of us.

Guess what, folks? The economy is not a pie. The economy is more like a fruit. You say, "A fruit? What are you talking about?" Well, a pie has a finite number of pieces.

If there are seven pieces of pie and I take one, there are only six left for whoever's left. If I take two of them there are only five left. What if I take six pieces of pie? Then there's only one left. If the economy is like a pie, it would mean the more money I make, the less money there is for everybody else. But that's not how life is; that's not how the economy really works. Nothing in nature works this way. It would take a person with a "Lack Mentality" to create such a system and it would take people with a "Lack Mentality" to buy into it. The economy doesn't work like this because the economy is not a pie.

Abundance Is Not Limited; It's Infinite

The difference is that people who believe in limited abundance truly believe that if they make too much, there won't be enough for other people. I believe that the more everybody makes, the more there is for everybody to make.

For instance, let's say that we come to an apple tree and it has a dozen apples on it. I take an apple and eat it. People with a lack of mentality would say, "Myron, there are less apples now because you ate the apple." I say, "No, there are potentially many more apples because I ate the apple. Because I'm going to take these six seeds in my hand and I'm going to plant them in the ground. They are going to become apple trees. Now I have six more apple trees and they each produce 100 apples a year. So because I ate the apple, in just a few years, there will literally be 600 more apples per year than there were before I ate the apple.

My understanding of infinite abundance is, because I make more money, the more there is for everybody to make,

For instance, when I used to be broke, I was so poor that poor people felt sorry for me. It was not uncommon for me to buy a car for $50 and drive it around. When I drove that $50 car, I never put it in the shop. I never took it to the car wash. I always washed it by hand. I never took it to the dealership to get serviced. I couldn't afford it. The only person that benefited from my $50 car was me and the person I gave $50 to.

Now I drive a brand new 2006 Mercedes CLS 500 Coupe and a 2006 Cadillac Escalade. Those cars cost considerably more than $50. I no longer wash my own cars. Now, I pay anywhere from $20 to $50 to have my cars washed. I never took my $50 car to a car wash, but now the car wash is making more money because I have more money.

Now, when my cars need servicing, I put them in the shop. Now the dealership makes more money. They also made more money when I bought the new cars. There are more people in the equation who are all making more money because I am. Everyone benefits.

Literally, everybody who comes in contact with me makes more money because I make more money. The economy really does work just like eating fruit off

The Ebony Treasure Map

of a tree. If you eat it and then you plant it, more grows. If I make more money and spend some of that money, everybody that I spend money with makes more money. Anybody can understand the concept of infinite abundance. The more you make, the more there is for everybody to make.

CHAPTER TWELVE

Since You Can't Beat 'Em, Join 'Em"

So many people have the philosophy of "us against them" because they have bought into this limited abundance philosophy. It's "the have nots against the haves".

My motto is why hate 'em? Don't be a hater, be a "participator". Don't be a hater be a "celebrator". Don't be somebody who hates rich people. Don't be somebody who despises wealth. Become somebody who creates wealth. Become the kind of person who is rich yourself, then you don't have to be a hater anymore, because then you realize there is more than enough for everybody.

You can never become wealthy if you are a person who hates wealthy people. You will not become something that you despise. So don't hate wealth and don't hate wealthy people, but join us. Become one of the elite. Become the kind of person who does the right things with their money to create income, so that you can become the kind of person that has control over your own future. Give yourself some choices by becoming wealthy. Since you can't beat 'em; join 'em.

We would love to have you join us on top of this great financial mountain. Remember, "there is plenty of room at the top of the economic heap, it's the bottom of the heap that's crowded". With that in mind I invite you to join me and millions of others who have made it to the top of the financial "Mount Everest"

CHAPTER THIRTEEN

You "Can" If Your Cans Say You Can

One of the most important factors in becoming rich is to have a money management system that tells you what to do with your money. You don't want to wait until you become rich to start managing your money. Start a money management system today. In this chapter I am going to lay out this simple yet powerful system for you. Follow it and you will become rich beyond your wildest imagination.

Don't forget, whether you are rich, poor, or middle class is not determined by how much money you make, but what you do with $1 when you get it.

I'm going to teach you what I call the "Money Management Principle of Millionaires" in this chapter. Follow this to the letter. The money management principle of millionaires teaches this philosophy: "Get all you CAN. CAN all you get." And your Cans mean you Can!

If you are very diligent and faithful about managing your money, your money will multiply. If you are haphazard in managing your money, your money will be gobbled up by the little foxes.

You "CAN" Manage Your Money

You say, "Myron, how do I manage my money?" I say, "Get all you CAN. CAN all you get. Your Cans mean you Can." I want you to go to a home improvement store. Go to Lowe's, Home Depot, or a hardware store, and get six paint cans: gallon, quart, or pint, it doesn't matter. Then I want you to divide your money into six different categories using these cans.

Can Number One: "I Can Tithe Can"

The first can is what I call your "I can tithe" can. Yes, I believe in tithing. I believe that you should tithe. I believe that you're not living off of 100% of your income, anyway, so you might as well tithe.

Tithing, in my opinion and from a Biblical perspective, is giving 10% of your gross income back to God's work through the church. I don't believe that tithing and charity are the same thing. (Understand that this is my opinion.) I know there are a lot of people that do give to charity for their tithe. That's ok. If that's what you believe.

I believe that tithing means you give back 10% to God, demonstrating that you trust Him as the one who provides for you. I believe that we can do a lot through our human effort, but I know for a fact that if God puts his blessing in the equation, then it will go to a completely different level. I like what Robert Allen and Mark Victor Hansen said in the book "The One Minute Millionaire": "God knows where the gold is." So your first can is your "I can tithe" can. Take 10% of your gross and put it in your "I can tithe" can. Every Sunday when you go to church, you take that money out of your "I can tithe" can and you put it in your church. Or send it to your favorite charity, if that is how you choose to do it.

Can Number Two: "I Can Finish Free Can"

Number two can is your "I can finish free" can. This is your can that you are going to use to invest in things that can produce passive streams of income for you. This is your "I can finish free" can.

Ten percent of your income goes into your "I can tithe" can. Ten percent of your income goes into your "I can finish free" can.

The money in your "I can finish free" can, you can never spend. Not now, not ten years from now, not 100 years from now, not 1000 years from now. You never spend the money you put in your "I can finish free" can. Instead of spending this money you buy businesses that can create passive income for you. You will be able to spend the profit that passive income creates for you.

So let's say that you eventually buy a Laundromat that costs you $350,000 from your "I can finish free" can and earns you $170,000 a year. While you own the Laundromat If you sell the Laundromat, you have to put that $350,000 back in the "I can finish free" can.

If you get started in a Network Marketing company, you can use the money from this can to pay for your monthly requirements until your Network Marketing business can pay it for you. When you start making money in your Network Marketing business, be sure to manage that money with your cans as well.

Can Number Three: "I Can Educate Myself"

The next can is your "I can educate myself" can. This is the can you use for personal development. Put

10% of your income in this can. This is what you use to go to seminars, buy audio programs, buy books, etc. This is the money you use to educate yourself in the areas of expertise in which you are developing.

Remember what I told you earlier in this book? One of the differences between rich people and poor people is that poor people entertain themselves and rich people educate themselves. Poor people spend a large amount of their money on entertainment, but rich people spend a large amount of their money on education. Keep in mind this is self-education, not necessarily higher education like college and grad school.

One of the biggest reasons I became wealthy is because for years, even when I was broke, even before I understood the money management principles of millionaires, I constantly invested in my own mind.

I've invested over $80,000 in my own self-education in the last 10 years. I've invested over $10,000 this year and it's July. I went to a marketing conference last month that cost me $1,295 to attend. While I was there, I bought another $5,000.00 worth of home study courses. I was able to do this not just because I am rich, but because of my "I can educate myself" can. This can, will pay for all of your personal development materials, workshops and seminars. It can even pay for all of your transportation and lodging.

You may be wondering "Why would you spend that kind of money?" Because the best investment you can make is not in real estate or the stock market. The best investment you will ever make will be the investment that you make into your own mind. The second best investment that you can make is the investment into your own business or businesses.

I urge you to invest in personal development. Not only do I invest in my own personal development, all my millionaire friends' number one category for investment is their own mind (through personal development). Remember, the most important investment you will ever make is the investment you make in your own mind. It always pays the highest returns.

Can Number Four: "I Can Save for What I Want Can"

You've got your "I can tithe" can. You've got your "I can finish free" can. You've got your "I can educate myself" can. Now you have your "I can save for what I want" can.

The "I can save for what I want" can may be used for several things. You put money in this to save for your vacation. If you want to buy a new car, you save up for your down payment. If you want to buy new furniture, you save up for your new furniture in your "I can save for what I want" can.

Also, if you have an emergency come up and the refrigerator goes out or the car breaks down, you use the money in this can for those kinds of expenses. This is your "I can save for what I want" can. If you want to go on a shopping spree, you save up your money in your "I can save for what I want" can.

Can Number Five: "I Can Have Fun Can"
The fifth can is one of my favorites. It's your "I can have fun" can. This can has a stipulation on it: you have to spend all of the money in your "I can have fun" can every month. This is the money that you blow every month on yourself doing something that you think is fun. I'm talking about a shopping spree if you love to shop. I'm talking about golf if you love golf. I'm talking about going out to eat at a fine restaurant, or a $200 massage. Whatever it is that you are into that is really fun for you. Use that money every month on fun activities.

That can right there will make you rich, because you want to make more money so you can put more and more and more money into your "I can have fun" can. This can will help you to conquer some of the "deserve issues" you may have. When you start blowing money on yourself, you start feeling like you are worth it. You also get used to having nice things and having nice things done for you. This can, will change your life.

Can Number Six: "I Can Pay My Bills Can"
That's five of the six cans. The last can is your "I can pay my bills can". Fifty percent of your money goes in this can. This is the money you use for your car payment, house payment, your utilities, your insurance, your food. This is the money that you use for your living expenses. This is your "I can pay my bills can". You pay all your monthly household expenses out of this can.

Are you thinking you can't live off of half of your income? If that is what you are thinking, don't worry. Here are a couple of things that you can do to fix this. Simplify your life. If you can't live off of half of your income, sell the car that you have to make payments on and buy a cheaper one that you can pay cash for. Downgrade your house. Do whatever you have to do to lower your monthly expenses.

If you are married, combine both incomes and then manage the money using the cans. If you don't want to keep cash in the cans, open a separate account for each category and keep the ledgers for each account in its own can. Get to the point where you can live off of half of your income. Use the money management principle of millionaires to get yourself over the top. The benefits of using the cans will start to show up in a very short period of time. Remember, "Get all you CAN, CAN all you get, and your CANS mean you can!"

Now that we've gone through all of the principles in The Ebony Treasure Map, we'll look at some treasure traps to avoid. Remember, on a treasure hunt there will be some traps that must be avoided in order to find your treasure.

There are twenty-six treasure traps that you have to avoid in order to be on your way to becoming wealthy. You can eliminate the pitfalls that keep most black people in poverty for their entire lives and even for future generations. We're going to look at thirteen Mental Treasure Traps and then we're going to look at thirteen Practical Treasure Traps.

CHAPTER FOURTEEN

13 Mental Treasure Traps That Can Keep You from Your Treasure

There are twenty-six Treasure Traps that you must avoid if you want to become wealthy. You can eliminate the pitfalls that keep most black people in poverty for their entire lives and even for future generations. We're going to look at thirteen Mental "Treasure Traps" and then we're going to look at thirteen Practical Treasure Traps.

The Thirteen Mental Treasure Traps

Mental Treasure Trap #1
Mistaking Negativism for Skepticism

The first Mental Treasure Trap that black people need to avoid is mistaking negativism for skepticism. Skepticism is good. Negativism is bad. You might ask, "What's the difference between skepticism and negativism?" Skepticism says, "I'm not sure that this is for real. I've got my doubts; however, I'm willing to check it out further. I'm going to investigate to find out whether my skepticism is valid or not."

Negativism says, "I don't think this is good and I'm not even going to look at it. I don't think there is any possibility of this happening, so it's not even worth looking into." That negativism will keep you in poverty your whole life. Be skeptical, but don't be negative.
When somebody offers you an opportunity to investigate an opportunity that could make you

financially independent, if the first words out of your mouth are, "It sounds too good to be true," stop right there. Just because it sounds too good to be true doesn't mean that it is too good to be true. The first thing that comes to your mind might be, "Well, if it's that easy, everyone would be doing it." How much do you think that kind of thinking has cost you in your life? Most people have those kind of thoughts and most people are broke. "It's easier to make a lot of money than it is to make a little bit."

While you may be skeptical or negative about that statement, I'm going to urge you to go ahead and investigate further. So when somebody offers you an opportunity to make large sums of money or offers you a chance to look at an opportunity whereby you can make large sums of money, be skeptical, but don't be negative. Don't be so negative that you won't even look at it.

I once had one of my millionaire friends tell me, "Myron, I tell you what, when somebody offers me an opportunity, I always look at it. Most of the time, I make up my mind that I'm not going to do it. However, I always, always look because I never know which opportunity that I pass up might be the one that could have made me a fortune." That makes really good sense. Always look. It doesn't cost you anything or require much energy to look. So my question is, "Why not look? Why not investigate?"

As a people, we need to stop mistaking our negativism for skepticism. Be skeptical, but don't be negative. When somebody offers you an opportunity to do anything that's going to make your life better, at least investigate. Don't just say, "No, that sounds too good to be true so it must not be true."

In one of my businesses, I give other people an opportunity to make money. I teach them how to do it. I literally take them by the hand and lead them into what I call the Financial Promised Land. The requirement is that they must be coachable and available.

In fact, I was speaking with a young lady at a bank recently and I said, "If there was a way for you to earn an extra $150,000 a year, would it be worth eight minutes of your time to check it out?" You know what she said? She said, "Well, you know, that sounds too good to be true." The fact is, if she had really thought about it instead of just reacting, she would have thought, "Obviously, what I think works has only gotten me to where I am right now. If this individual is telling me they've got an opportunity for me to make $150,000 a year, it might not be true, but if it is, I don't want to leave it behind," instead of just saying, "Well, it sounds too good to be true," or "If it was that easy, everyone would be doing it." That's a mistake that most people make. Remember, your current understanding is producing your current results. If you want some new results, you must get a new understanding.

Mental Treasure Trap #2
Being Too Myopic About Money

Another Mental Treasure Trap we face is that we are too myopic around the subject of money. The word myopic means we only see things that are up close and not things that are down the road. We don't look at tomorrow. We don't look at next week. We don't look

The Ebony Treasure Map

at next month. We don't look at ten years from now. All of our financial planning is around the next five minutes. That is a major Treasure Trap that keeps black people from being financially independent.

We only do those things financially that feel good to us right now. We do hardly any long-term planning. We don't look down the road to next week, next month, and next year. Five years from now, ten years from now, twenty years from now, one hundred years from now, after we're gone, what kind of legacy will we leave our children? Have we made the world a better place because we were here? We don't even look at that because we don't think it's important. We don't see it as a crisis—it's not something that has to be handled right now.

Right now was five years from now five years ago. We just never stop to think about it. While we may not be able to do anything to solve the crisis we're in right now, we can make our tomorrow better than today. We can do this by preparing better today for tomorrow, than we did yesterday for today.

I heard a man say once, "You are what you have been becoming." That is a powerful statement. "You are right now what you have been becoming." You are financially, mentally, spiritually, and physically what you have been becoming. You are the sum total of your past days. Guess what? Your future will be the sum total of your present days and you will be what you are becoming right now.

So let me ask you a question. What are you becoming? Don't be so myopic that you think your whole life exists in the next five minutes. Look down the road farther than that. Become somebody who plans into the future.

I read in a book once, "We better spend some time preparing for our future because we are going to spend the rest of our lives there." Think about that for a minute. We better spend some time preparing for our future because we're going to spend the rest of our lives there.

In the Bible, Solomon was the wealthiest and wisest man in the world. He said, "Go to the ant, thou sluggard; consider her ways, and be wise: which having no guide, or overseer, or ruler, provideth her meat in the summer, and gathereth her food in the harvest." Solomon said if you don't want to be poor your whole life, you've got to be like an ant. An ant thinks winter all summer and an ant thinks summer all winter. That's why an ant does so well. He's working constantly. In the winter time he's working to get ready for the summertime. He's working because he knows it's not always going to be cold.

It's not always going to be as hard as it is right now. You may be in the winter of your life right now. Work like you know summer is coming. There's going to come a time when you can bask in the sun. There's going to come a time when you won't be working just to make ends meet. There's going to come a time when you're going to actually have treasure to enjoy and time to enjoy your money and money to enjoy your time, but you've got to be like an ant. You've got to think summer all winter. Just because things are bad right now, don't go through life thinking things are always going to be like they are right now. They're not.

The Ebony Treasure Map

At the end of every night, there's a day. At the end of every winter, there's a spring. I've only been here forty-five years, but every single solitary winter I've ever been through has been followed by a spring. The ant thinks summer all winter, but he doesn't just think summer all winter. He doesn't just think positive when things are negative, but the ant thinks negative when things are positive. In other words, the ant thinks winter all summer. When it's summertime, the ant doesn't just say, "It's summertime, I'm just going to chill. I'm just going to take my time. I'm just going to hang out. I'm just going to watch TV and play PlayStation. It's summer. Everything is good. We've got plenty of food. We don't have anything to worry about. We're just going to have a good time."

That's not what the ant does. The ant says, "Ok, it's summertime right now, but winter is coming. I've got to work. Winter is coming. I've got to prepare. Winter is coming. I've got to get ready. Winter is coming." Others will say, "Why are you working so hard, man? Don't you see the sun shining? Let's go play and hang out." But you can't listen to your summertime friends because winter is coming. You've got to make sure you're ready when the cold weather comes.

Don't be so myopic that you fall in the Ebony Treasure Trap of only seeing today, today. You've got to learn how to see tomorrow, today, if you want to become wealthy. That's Mental Treasure Trap Number Two that keeps black folks from becoming wealth

Mental Treasure Trap #3
We Don't Desire or Like Money

You say, "Yes, I do. I desire money. I want to be able to pay my light bill." Yes, that's what I'm talking about. You don't really desire it because if the only thing you want money for is to pay your light bill, then your payday is not really a payday anyway; it's just a transfer day. So you are only making money to pay it to someone else, you are not using it to create wealth. All you're doing is running back and forth, working hard to pay the light bill and pay the house payment and pay the water bill and pay the food bill. You're not really earning a living. You're just transferring money from the person who employs you to the person you owe. Unfortunately, as a people, we have bought into the philosophy that money is inherently evil. We don't like money. We only want to make enough to get by.

In fact, if you ask a person, "What's your plan for becoming rich?" Oftentimes, black folks: men, women, boys, and girls say, "You know, I don't want to be rich. I just want to make enough to get by." Well, why would you just want to make enough to get by? Why would you want to survive when you could thrive? You want to do more than get by. You want to create wealth so you can make a difference in the world around you.

You want to create wealth so you can influence the other generations of young black people who are coming after us, who are right now being influenced by the drug culture and by the gangster culture and by the culture that only wants to exploit them when it could empower them.

So, yes, you should want to become wealthy. Don't just say, "Ya know, I don't really like money. It's really not that important to me." If it's not that important to you, you'll never have lots of it. Who is going to go through life figuring out ways to get lots of something that is not that important to them? Some people say, "Well, being rich isn't everything." Don't minimize becoming rich; emphasize it and celebrate it.

That whole mentality started in the slave culture. White slave masters wanted black people to believe that they didn't deserve anything on this side. They wanted them to believe that everything good they would get after they died. The Bible doesn't promote or support that way of thinking. In fact the Bible promotes the exact opposite.

Here is what I mean. Jesus said, "I am come that you might have life and that you might have it more abundantly." That's not just talking about "after awhile." That's talking about right now. All the great patriarchs of the Bible were wealthy. All the prominent people in the New Testament owned businesses. They were not employees. They were not employees in the corporate slavery. They had their own businesses.

Some of you may be thinking, "Money is the root of all evil." It's not. The Bible says, "The *love* of money is the root of all evil." It doesn't say money is the root of all evil.

Understand what that passage means. "The love of money is the root of all evil." It doesn't mean it's the root of every evil in the whole wide world to the exclusion of no evil. "The love of money is the root of all evil" means the love of money is the root of all kinds, all sorts, all types, and all manner of evil. The word "all" in the New Testament seldom means "all to the exclusion of none." Usually what the word "all" means in Scripture is "all kinds, all types, all manner". What it means is that the love of money is all kinds of evil.

In other words, people will do all kinds of evil things to get money. It is not saying, if you love money, that makes you evil. That's not what it's talking about. If you're going to use that Bible verse, or if you are going to start promoting something as Bible doctrine or you're going to use it to prove your point, you might as well think about what it means instead of assigning your own meaning to it.

So don't hate and despise money. Don't get to the place where you don't like or desire money. You may be wondering, "Myron, how much money should I want to make?" I'm going to tell you the exact amount of money you should want to make, down to the penny. You should make as much as you possibly can. That's the exact number. If you can become a billionaire, you don't want to just become a millionaire. If you want to become a millionaire, you don't want to make just fifty-thousand dollars a year. You want to earn as much money as you can.

I know that you may be one of the people who is wondering how I could say something like that?" Think about it. A tree grows as tall as it can. A dog barks as loud as it can. A cheetah runs as fast as it can. The wind blows as hard as it can. Human beings are the only creatures in nature that do less than we can and that's because we have a choice. Since we have a choice, let's choose to do as much as we can instead of doing less than we can. Let's not live our lives only half full. Some people say, "Well, you know, I've lived ninety years." But what they have really done is lived ten years and repeated it nine times. Some people haven't grown since they were nine years old. So many people never learn any new skill. Many never learn any new information. The sad thing is these very same people go to the grave thinking that their limited view of things is just the way things are.

Don't just live the same year over and over again. People say, "Well, I've got twenty years of experience in business." But they really don't have twenty years of business experience; they really just have one year of experience in business and they've repeated it twenty times. There is a huge difference. Don't despise money. Desire it. Earn as much as you can so you can make as big a difference as you can.

Don't say, "I just want to make a lot of money so I can help other people." Not that there's anything wrong with helping other people, but you want to do more than just help other people. You want to wear nice clothes, drive a nice car, take great vacations and live in a nice house. So don't say "I only want to make money so I can help other people." There's nothing wrong with making money so you can help other people, but help yourself too. Yes, I drive a nice car. Yes, I wear nice clothes. Yes, I have nice jewelry. Yes, I like nice things. And because I make so much more money than the average person, I can also do a lot more to help others. But I want to do more than just help other people; I want to live the best life possible for me. And so do you, so stop trying to fake everybody out.

Don't despise money. That's the third Mental Treasure Trap: So avoid it like the plague!

Mental Treasure Trap # 4
We Despise Ourselves & Anyone Who Looks Like Us.

I'm talking to black people in particular, because we are the only people I know of who despise ourselves and anybody who looks like us. It's amazing. We are so self-despising. It's tragic, but that's what our ancestors were taught to do in slavery. In fact, I travel at least three weekends a month. Sometimes I travel four or even five weekends a month. When I am at the airport or at the mall, and I see other African Americans, many of my people won't even look at me so I can say hello. Don't just take my word for it. Check it out for yourself.

We, as a people, don't trust each other enough to look each other in the eye and say, "Hello." That's tragic. "Well, I'm afraid if I say hello to that woman, she might think I'm flirting with her." Or maybe a woman of color might think, "I'm afraid if I say hello to that man, he might think I'm flirting with him." If you are an African American man have you ever had this thought: "I'm afraid that if I look at that brother, he might look at me and think, "Punk, what you looking at"?

The fact is, it's ok to look at each other. We don't have to despise each other. We even refer to each other in derogatory terms that slave masters made up for our people. I don't use the word "niggah." I don't allow my children to use that word. You know why? Because that's not what we are; we are a great people that God put greatness in just like He put greatness in other folks.

I love America. In fact, I wouldn't want to live anywhere else. Even though I love America, I recognize she hasn't always loved me and my ancestors. The fact that we have even survived as a people in America is amazing. If you have survived, even if you're in the lowest depths of poverty right now as an African American, you have greatness inside of you just because you have survived. If you've gone beyond survival and have thrived, you really ought to know you have greatness inside of you. Don't despise yourself. Don't despise your own people.

When you have the opportunity to do business with a black man or a black woman, do it. We're the only people in the world who prefer to do business with somebody outside our race. You know what's tragic about it? The more educated we become, the worse we despise ourselves and the more we try to be something that we are not. What we need to do is go ahead and accept that fact that "I am a brother," or "I am a sister." Don't just accept that fact; embrace it. Celebrate it. We as a people have thrived in every arena we have ever set our foot into.

For a long time we weren't even allowed to step in certain arenas because we supposedly weren't good enough, we weren't smart enough, we weren't physically capable enough. But when you look at all the great things that have been discovered and created, you'll see that many of them were discovered and created by these people who supposedly weren't good enough.

The Ebony Treasure Map

We ought to recognize the greatness in ourselves when we remember that the first wristwatch that was made in America with all American parts was made by a black mathematician named Benjamin Banneker. The first successful open heart surgery was done by a black man. The greatest basketball player who ever lived is a black man named Michael Jordan. The greatest golfer of all time, right now, is a black man by the name of Tiger Woods. One of the greatest tennis players was Arthur Ashe. The greatest female tennis players are the Williams sisters. I am not saying that black people as a race are superior to other races. I am saying that we are not inferior as we have been made to believe. We can compete in any arena and at any level if we put our minds to it.

Since we excel in every arena we step into, why shouldn't we put our feet into the arena of capitalism? Why shouldn't we seek out treasure, so that we can be blessed and bless our people and make the world a better place because we were here? Why should we not step into the arena of becoming millionaires and billionaires? Is it because we have believed the lie that has been propagated to us that we're not good enough, not smart enough, not strong enough, don't have enough character or enough this or enough that? When somebody in our race does do something exceptional, other folks say, "They're special. They're different than other black people." No, we are what we are. Don't believe for a minute that success is something out of the ordinary for us. Success is our natural way of being.

Sometimes we find the greatness inside of us that God placed in us and we manifest it. Other times we don't find it because we've been blinded to this. We don't like ourselves and we don't like anybody who looks like us. Well, I like us. I like me. I like brothers and sisters who look like me. I like other folks too. One of the reasons I do like other people is because I like me and my people. If I didn't like me, I couldn't like anyone else because I wouldn't have the capacity to do so. Understand this. This is not something against white people, but this is something for black people. There's a huge difference. When you understand how we've been kicked around as a people, then you understand why we need to hear this message that I'm giving right now. If we're going to become wealthy, we must stop despising ourselves. We must start respecting ourselves and other people who look like us.

Mental Treasure Trap #5
We Value Consumption More Than We Value Production

This is one principle that can make you wealthy, even if you only have a job. Learn to value production over consumption. I am talking about production versus consumption when it comes to how you use your money. You may be wondering. "What's the difference between production and consumption?" Production means you use your money to produce more money instead of using your money to consume someone else's product. Every time you make money, you make sure that money produces something before you just spend it. Don't just use your money to consume things.

Most people make the mistake of thinking that money is only for spending. That's why people say things like, "Why would I want to make more money than I can spend?" If that is how you think, I know that you're broke. When you say things like, "I just want to make enough to get by," I know you're in poverty.

You should not use money just as something to spend. . In fact, you should not be spending more than half of your money on your bills. However much you're making right now, if that's how much your bills require, if it takes all of your money to live right now, there are two things you need to work on: you must work on cutting your expenses in half and you need to work on doubling your income.. How do you do it? You do it by becoming a producer rather than just a consumer.

Most of our people have the mentality that causes them to think they have to have every nice thing they see. "I've got to have these $200 shoes and these $70 jeans," and on and on it goes. Not that there is anything wrong with having those things. But there is something wrong with using the money that you should use for financial freedom to buy those things. Don't be just a consumer. Don't just look for the name brand stuff or spend extra money to put somebody else's name on your clothes (by this I mean logo and brand). Use your money to become a rich, and then you can buy anything you want.

We've been programmed to be consumers as opposed to producers by the media. Television, radio, newspapers, and magazines are all succeeding in programming us to be consumers. Not to mention the videos, the MTV, the BET, and more, have programmed us for massive consumption. The media is a tool that has been used to exploit us for the profits of others. We buy into their messages and become bigger and bigger consumers and have less and less.

One of the problems we have is that we spend tomorrow's income on today's luxuries. We spend the money to buy things that make us look like we are something that we'll never be, because we use all of our resources trying to look like we're successful. I would rather be a millionaire who doesn't look like a millionaire than look like a millionaire and not be one. Treasure Trap Number Five is we value consumption more than we value production. Become a producer and you will have the ability to consume the nicest things in life, multiply your income, and cut your expenses all at the same time.

Mental Treasure Trap #6
We Don't Trust Or Like People With Money Unless They're Exploiting Us

Often when a black man or a black woman sees another black man or woman driving a nice car or wearing a nice suit of clothes, they despise them and think, "They think they're somebody" or "They've done something illegal or immoral to get it." Or they may look at them and say, "I don't know who they think they are. They think they are so much because they've got …"

We must learn to respect people and celebrate their successes instead of being jealous, envious, and despising people just because they have money. In fact, if you were to ask the average poor person, "How much money is too much?" They would usually tell you something more than the amount they have. It doesn't matter if they're making $30,000 a year or $50,000 a year or $70,000 a year, but they would tell you that too much money is more than they have. If you want to become wealthy, you cannot despise wealthy people.

The only wealthy people that poor people don't despise are the ones that exploit them. The ones who utilize the fact that they are a consumer and very consumptive by nature and they use that against them.

Here's how I look at life. If you buy something from me, it ought to add value to your life. If it doesn't, then I have done you a disservice. I want to add value to everybody I come in contact with and certainly anyone I do business with. I want to add massive, massive value. In order for that to take place, in order for you to recognize your poverty programming, you're going to want to attend one of our Six-Figure Business Schools. There, we teach you all kinds of great marketing techniques. We teach you about how to own a business. We teach you how to think like a business owner. We teach you how to explode your business. We teach you many, many different ways to generate income.

But at the Six-Figure Business School, one of the most important things we do is extract your poverty programming from you. You can't become wealthy if you don't trust or like people who are wealthy unless they are exploiting you. We as a people have a tendency to respect those that exploit us but not the people who add real value.

Mental Treasure Trap #7
We Are Techno Phobic Or Least Techno Ignorant.

I always feel sorry for our people when they say, "Well, I don't have a computer." "Or I don't know how to use a computer". You have a television. Sell your television and buy a used computer. You say, "Well, I wouldn't get that much for my television." Sell all of your televisions. Even if you don't get that much for the television, you will be better off without it until you learn to create wealth. I know that this is some pretty radical stuff. And the poorer you are, the more difficult it is for you to imagine giving up your television. A television is an electronic income reducer.

When I was poor, I got rid of my television until I wasn't poor any more. Until I got over the addiction to being broke, I got rid of my television. I have noticed that being addicted to television and being addicted to being broke go hand in hand. I got rid of my television and my financial picture turned around. I wanted to make sure that I supplied a great living for my family and left a legacy for my grandchildren and my great-grandchildren. So I'm going to encourage you to do the same thing. Don't just get caught up in television and be techno phobic.

We're so techno phobic, we don't know how to use the Internet. We don't have high speed Internet. Get a computer. Get high speed Internet. Learn how to make money online. You say, "I don't know how to do that." Good. Come to one of our Six-Figure Business Schools and we'll share some of that information with you.

Most people don't understand that you can become wealthy selling other people's products. Believe it or not, there are people who make over $100,000 a year and they don't even have a product to sell! They do it through affiliate programs or by driving traffic to other people's websites. I've got one guy who makes hundreds of dollars a month driving traffic to my website. He doesn't have to worry about delivery of product or fulfillment of product.

Well, guess what, folks? You can do that same exact thing. You can create wealth by becoming an affiliate for different websites out there and selling other people's products. You don't even have to have your own product to sell. Don't be techno phobic.
You don't know how to use a computer. I'm going to tell you something. Because of computer technology, because of the Internet, a person can literally operate a million dollar business right out of their home with a desktop or laptop computer and a little bit of software.

For example, if you want to create a music CD, you no longer have to rent a studio and buy expensive sound equipment. You can now create a professional sounding CD in your basement with a good computer and a program like Sound Forge, Vegas, Reason, or Pro Tools. You can also create books now much more cheaply than before. You can even produce a music video with a $1,000 camera and your computer. You no longer have to spend tons of money to create these products.

For example, a friend of mine and I started a record label. He's a brilliant musician. We started this record label to write and create songs that help people become wealthy. If you want to hear some clips from some of those songs, you can go to our music website www.inpowermentrecords.com. There you can listen to some song clips from our first album. These songs we created for conferences, for entrepreneurs and for people who want to become wealthy, to give them something to listen to that would empower them instead of disempowering them.

If you want to become wealthy, Treasure Trap number 7 that you need to avoid is don't be techno phobic or techno ignorant. I've created programs on my personal computer that have made me a fortune. They have made me six figures in a month, six figures in a week, tens of thousands of dollars a day, tens of thousands of dollars an hour. This would not be possible if it were not for the leverage of computers.

Don't be techno phobic. Learn how to use a computer. Learn how to use a conference call line. Develop your own conference call to teach people what you have learned. Develop something that teaches people how to make their lives better in some way, shape or form, and they will gladly pay you for it. Learn how to use a computer to develop or create something. Learn how to use the computer to sell something. Become the friend of technology and technology will be your friend.

Mental Treasure Trap # 8
We Value Security More Than We Value Freedom

This treasure trap is a big one. Security and freedom are not the same thing. I like what Helen Keller said. She was both blind and mute. She wrote "Security does not exist in all of nature. Neither do the sons of man as a whole experience it. Life is either a daring

The Ebony Treasure Map

adventure or nothing at all." I want to ask you a question today. What is your life? Is it a daring adventure or is it nothing at all?

Let me ask you another question. What is your life becoming? Is it becoming a daring adventure or is it becoming nothing at all? If you feel your life is "nothing at all", it doesn't have to stay that way. Your life can be more exciting than an action adventure movie.

Back when I was driving that trash truck during the day, I was reading books in the evening like "How to Master the Art of Selling Anything", "The Greatest Salesman of the World", "The University of Success Unlimited", "The Richest Man in Babylon", "Million Dollar Habits" and on and on. The books that I was reading and the tapes that I was listening to were changing who I was so I could create freedom for myself and my family. I was expanding my mind so that I wouldn't have to be stuck with a blue collar job or in corporate America my whole life. I went from being the trash man to being the cash man because I valued freedom and independence over security.

Benjamin Franklin said, "If you seek security, you have no independence." I want to be free. I am more interested in freedom than security. Most people are more interested in security than freedom and that's why they stay trapped at a job they hate their whole life because they are afraid that they're going to lose their security.

I'm going to tell you something. The security that you have is really not security. It's just a false sense of security. If you don't believe me, ask the 30,000 people who were laid off by Ford Motor Company whether or not they have security. Many of them were probably working for Ford for decades. Yet now they don't have a job. Why? These people find themselves in this unfortunate circumstance because they value security over independence and freedom.

America is known as the land of the free and the home of the brave, but how many people do you know who are really free? I mean really free. I don't want to just live in the land of the free; I want to be free in the land of the free. I have financial freedom. I have time freedom. I literally can wake up and have a brand new day that's like a blank canvas and I can paint on that canvas anything that I choose. Why? I live this reality because I valued freedom over security. When you get to the place where you value freedom over security, you can get to the point where you are financially independent, financially free, and not seeking financial security.

Mental Treasure Trap # 9
We Value Formal Education Over Self Education

We have bought into the formal education game. If a person is going to be a doctor, a lawyer, an engineer or something that requires a formal education, then I'm all for it. In fact, I submit to you, the educational system in America does not teach financial independence. It does not teach you how to think; it programs you not to think.

Don't get me wrong, it's very important to get an education. We must all learn to read and write and do arithmetic. But we must not make the mistake of thinking that education equals success. Because education doesn't equal success, success equals success. Until and unless a person learns to use his/her mind for the purpose of thinking, too much education can be more of a hindrance than help. The educational process often thwarts the greatness of our young people and thwarts the greatness of black people, because we're buying into the fact that more and more education makes you better or more likely to succeed. People think that having a degree means they deserve to make more money. Many people become disappointed when they graduate from college and cannot find a job that pays them what they had hoped they would earn when they started school.

People in their 30's and 40's and 50's and 60's are going back to school because their life isn't working. Well, guess what? It's not going to work any better after they go back to school. The formal educational process in this country thwarts intelligence and it thwarts the ability to think. Do you remember being in elementary school and the teacher teaching you how to do math equations? Do you remember being intimidated by math even at an early age? I believe most people struggle with math because when we talk about mathematical equations, we call them math problems.

Who wants a problem? Who wants to think about a problem? So, their mind shuts down and gives them a negative connotation of math before they even get started. If you're not good at math, you won't be good at money.

Go ahead and think back to the elementary school days. Your teacher taught you how to do mathematical equations. You understood the concept and figured out a better, easier, and faster way to do it. They said, "No, I don't want you to do it that way. I want you to do it this way." If two plus two is four, then what difference does it make how you get there? One of the negative things that comes from the way they teach math in schools is that you begin to believe on a subconscious level that, "in order for an answer to be right, it has to be hard".

The educational system doesn't want you to think. It just wants you to parakeet. It wants you to regurgitate what you have heard. The system doesn't want you to understand concepts; it only wants you to memorize processes. What can this prepare you for, besides being an employee?

Why does the educational system teach this way? Number one, that's how the teacher was taught to teach it. So if you do it a different way, you're not validating their education. Number two, if you do it a different way, you're causing them to have to think about what you just did. They don't have time to think. They're too busy processing papers according to their system. The current educational system doesn't teach you to think. It programs you not to think.

A good friend of mine, Jerry Clark, of www.clubrhino.com, said when he was in elementary school, the teacher said, "Columbus discovered America in 1492 and when he discovered America there were these people here and he called them Indians because they reminded him of the people he saw in India." He said he raised his hand and said, "Excuse me, teacher. I thought you said that Columbus discovered America." She said, "He did." Then Jerry said, "I thought you said there were people already here. If there were people already here, how could you say that he discovered it?"

He got sent to the principal's office. Why did Jerry get sent to the principal's office? Jerry got sent to the office because he was thinking. Not only did the teacher not want him to think, but the teacher didn't want to think either. The educational process in America does not teach you to think, it programs you not to think.

The educational process also creates a class system. I'm talking about smart versus dumb. What happens? You're in the classroom and the teacher calls you up to the board to work on a "math problem." You work it out and you get the wrong answer. What do all the other kids do in the classroom? They laugh. Not only do they laugh in the classroom, but when they get out on the playground, they call you a dummy and they call you stupid because you didn't know the answer.

Then what happens? You hit them and you get sent to the principal's office and get labeled as a bully. This whole process started because you pushed somebody around who had pushed you around first because the teacher taught them that it's ok for them to push you (by laughing), but it's not ok for you to push them (by hitting). You see what has happened? They've created a class system. This class system of smart versus dumb is a very difficult thing for children to process when they are just getting started in life.

You might even get labeled. What if you have a teacher who is an auditory teacher and you're a visual learner? Or you have a visual teacher and you're a kinesthetic learner? You learn by doing something, but the teacher expects you to learn just by saying something. It doesn't make you a bad person just because you don't learn the way they teach.

It's really interesting to me that the government forces children to go to school. The teachers are paid for being there. When the student can't learn the way the teacher teaches, we say the student has a learning disability. In my opinion, we ought to say that the teacher has a teaching disability because as a teacher, it should be the teacher's responsibility to cause every student in the class to learn what they're saying. After all, they are getting paid to teach.

Einstein said. "If I can't explain a concept to an intelligent twelve year old, I don't understand it myself." What if every teacher had that philosophy? What would happen in schools if the teachers took responsibility for what the child learns? What if the educational system admitted that if they can't explain a concept to a twelve year old, they don't understand it themselves?

We value formal education too much. I want you to think about this. Most college professors only know how to teach. They teach business, but if they knew how to do business, they'd have one. In order for that college business professor to be a great professor, they have to be an entrepreneur, either now or in the past. They would have to be a business owner in order to understand the nuances and the ins and outs and true concepts of being an entrepreneur and creating wealth. For somebody to teach personal finance, they have to be financially wealthy. You can't just teach something that you learned in a book. If you transfer something from your head, it will only reach the head, but if you transfer it from the heart, it will reach the heart. If you transfer it from your life, it will reach a whole life.

One of the problems with Treasure Trap #9 is that we value formal education over self education. You say, "Myron, what is self education?" Self education is the kind of education that I've given myself. My library is worth about $80,000 to $110,000. I invest in my mind on a monthly basis anywhere from $700-$5,000, sometimes a little more. I invest that much in self education because it manifests itself in fortune. Now I am not suggesting that you start out with that much of an investment, but start investing something in your mind.

I like what Jim Rohn said. "If you get a formal education, it will make you a living, but if you get a self education, it will make you rich." Formal education will make you a living, but self education will make you wealthy. While I heard Jim Rohn put this into words, I have proved it over and over in my own life.

The greatest things that I've ever learned in my life financially, I learned as an adult by buying a book, going to seminar, or buying an audio program and listening to it over and over again. Start a success library. Invest in your success library every month. Always learn something new that can make your life better. Don't be afraid of the challenge of learning something new. The new thing that you learn can create for you a new future and some new friends. So if you will go to work on yourself, your new self will go to work on your situation, and before you know it, you'll be living the life that you always dreamed about.

Remember, formal education will make you a living, but a self education can make you a fortune.

Mental Treasure Trap # 10
We Have No Financial Education

We don't understand how money works. I always say, "Any financial principle that you do not understand and you're not using, someone is using it against you." Therefore, it would behoove all of us to get as great a financial education as we possibly can. Most black people have no idea how money works.

We don't understand the Rule of 72. We don't understand how to use debt to create wealth; we only know how to use debt to create poverty. I know I have covered some of these topics in this book. I want you to make sure that what you've learned about financial principles in this book is the beginning of your financial literacy study and not the end of it.

If you want to be financially free, you must learn to use financial principles and keep some of all you earn and let that money earn more money for you. So you've got to take some of your money, at least ten percent of your money, and put it in a no-touch fund. You've got to put it in what I call my "I Can Finish Free" can. That ten percent of your income will literally change your life forever because you're putting it in something that you never take it out of, and you focus on putting that money in places that produce compound interest for you, a compound return for you. If you'll do that, then you'll be wealthy before you know it. I cannot emphasize enough the power of using the cans. If you haven't gotten your cans already, make sure you get them today and start managing your money.

After you finish with this book, go on to read other financial books that will teach you how to make your money work harder and harder for you. Make sure you continue your financial education and your wealth will continue to grow.

Mental Treasure Trap # 11
We Don't Understand And Utilize The Power Of Principles.

Most people, especially in our community, live life sort of haphazardly. We seem to think that becoming wealthy has something to do with luck or inheritance. It's got a whole lot more to do with principles than it does with luck.

I'm talking about the kind of principles that can make you wealthy beyond measure. Here's what I've discovered. All principles always work the same for everybody. All principles are microcosms of each other. If I implement the same principles in my finances that a wealthy person does, then I'm going to become wealthy. If I implement the same principles to my finances that a poor person does, then I'm going to be poor.

Don't forget the two-sentence wealth formula. If you want to be rich, Step #1 is "Find out what rich people do and do the same thing financially." Step # 2 is "Find out what poor people do and whatever else you do, don't do that." Again, all principles always work the same for everybody.

Here is a principle for you. Surround yourself with the people you want to be like. Because you are like the people you surround yourself with. Your income is not going to exceed that of your closest friends. If your closest friends are broke, then you're broke. If you want to change your income, one of the things you can do is just change your friends. I don't mean you have to get rid of them as friends, but you need to surround yourself with people who are doing better than you are. Those people will influence you in a totally different way than the people who are influencing you right now. If you want to become wealthy, get around wealthy people and start studying them. Buy books written by wealthy people and study those books and apply those principles to your life and you will achieve the same results. The people you surround yourself with will either pull you up or pull you down. Base your life on these principles and watch the effect it has on your income.

Mental Treasure Trap # 12
We Have A Renter's Mentality Versus An Owner's Mentality

This is so tragic. Other folks have figured out that we will rent anything. We will rent our house forever instead of buying one. Paying rent is like putting money down a black hole. You might be thinking, "I don't have good enough credit to buy a house." Well, get your credit fixed and buy your house and get paid to live there instead of paying to live there.

You live in a house and you pay $1,000 a month in rent and live there for five years. In that period, you've paid $60,000 to live in that house. When you move, you might get your $1,000 deposit back, but if you buy that same house, even if it costs you $150,000, and you live there for five years, you're going to get at least forty percent of your money back. Plus, the mortgage is going to be paid down, which means that all of the money you spent on that house you will get back in the form of equity and appreciation.

Renters have no equity or appreciation. Please stop renting a house. Buy a house. Get some creative financing and buy a house, but don't rent a house your whole life and end up with nothing. Creative financing is buying a house in a non-conventional way. Look for an owner of a house who is a "motivated seller" (maybe they got a job transfer or maybe they have to move to take care of a sick relative). When people find themselves in a situation like this, when they have to sell the house NOW, they will often finance the house for you. You would give them a down payment (usually much less than a traditional down payment) and make payments to them and they pay their mortgage company. Understand this principle. Don't have a renter's mentality. Don't live in an apartment your whole life unless, of course, you happen to own the apartment building and then you get paid to live there.

Not only do we rent houses, we rent furniture. Please black people, please stop renting furniture. You end up paying more for the furniture than it was worth and have nothing at the end. It doesn't make any sense. They get you on the monthly payment scam. Don't buy into the monthly payment scam or the weekly payment scam with renting furniture. It will keep you in poverty your whole life. You'll own nothing. You'll never have any equity in anything.

Now it's gotten so bad that they've got these little places called Rent and Roll where people rent rims for their car. The rims are worth more than the car. They want to rent rims so they can look like somebody. Don't do that. If you can't go down and pay cash for rims for your car, don't even buy rims for your car. Just keep the wheels on it that are already there. Don't take your future wealth and spend it on frivolous nonsense. Get rid of your renter's mentality and get an ownership mentality.

Mental Treasure Trap # 13
We're Against What Is For Us, And We're For What's Against Us

As a people, we are for what's against us and we're against what's for us. Think about it. Isn't that a tragedy? If something is against us, we're for it. We eat the worst possible foods and we make fun of people who eat foods that support life. We literally are for what's against us and we're against what's for us. In fact, we trust people we shouldn't trust and don't trust people we should. This trap sums up all of the previous traps in this chapter. If you want to get the most out of this book, then make sure you examine every aspect of your life. Ask yourself the question, "Am I what is for me or against me in this situation"?

Be for what's for you and against what's against you and not the other way around and you can avoid these Treasure Traps. Now we're going to go on to the

The Ebony Treasure Map

next thirteen Treasure Traps and those are the Practical Treasure Traps of black people.

CHAPTER FIFTEEN

Thirteen Practical Treasure Traps That Can Keep You from Your Fortune

Practical Treasure Trap #1
We Don't Protect Our Minds

We don't protect our minds from people who want to exploit us for our money and our minds. You can be free in your body and a slave in your mind. You can be a slave to your appetite. You can be a slave to pleasure. You can be a slave to sleep. You can be a slave to food. You can be a slave to spending money on stuff that you don't need. You can be a slave to so many different things if you don't protect your mind and you let just anyone in there.

Be very careful what you allow to go into your mind because once it gets in there you cannot control or change what it does to you. But, remember you can control what gets in there in the first place. Often it is the subtle messages that get into your mind that have a more damaging affect than the overt messages.

Practical Treasure Trap #2
We Don't Invest In Our Greatest Asset: Our Mind

I already covered this in the section on the money management principles of millionaires and having the "I can educate myself" can. It is a huge mistake to not invest in your mind.

Remember what Benjamin Franklin said, "If you empty your purse into your mind, your mind will fill your purse with gold." I say that whoever puts the most money in your mind, that's who has most of your money.

That's why most poor people and most poor African-Americans spend most of their money buying stuff that makes them look like they have something that they will never have because they are so busy trying to look like they have it. Treasure Trap #2 is we don't invest in our greatest asset, which is our mind. This a good time for me to re-establish the I Can Educate Myself Can. Make sure you have a can for self education and make sure you are constantly investing in books, seminars and home study courses that can make you a fortune.

Practical Treasure Trap #3
We Have No Financial Assets

We only own financial wealth reducing liabilities. We only own things that take money out of our financial house. We don't own anything that puts money in our financial house without us working for that money. That is a huge, huge financial Treasure Trap. If all you spend money on is stuff that costs you money after you buy it, you will be broke for the rest of your life, or at least until you change that habit.

A life change happened for me when my focus changed from buying wealth reducing liabilities to buying income producing assets. An asset is anything that brings money into your financial house without you working for the money. You have to start building assets. I recommend that you start with your own business. If you don't have a business, get back with the person who recommended this book to you, I'm sure they have a great business opportunity to share with you. If they can't help you get started in a business, then call my office and we will have one of our business partners call you and assist you in getting started in a business. Avoid the trap of going another day without having something in your income producing asset window.

Practical Treasure Trap #4
We Entertain Ourselves More Than We Educate Ourselves.

I covered this in several sections of this book already. So I'm not going to go into great detail, but I'm going to say this again in the section on Treasure Traps: I believe that if you are financially challenged that you cannot afford to watch television. My definition of financially challenged is anybody who makes less than $20,000 a month. You cannot afford to watch television because that amount of time spent in entertainment means you've got that many more people putting money into your mind than you are. If you can't make yourself get rid of your television set, then at least don't watch it for a month and use the time you used to spend watching TV on reading and listening to educational CDs. See what happens for you after 30 days. Break the entertainment habit and replace it with the education habit and watch great things begin to happen in your life.

Practical Treasure Trap # 5
We Are Paralyzed By A Paycheck
Most people can never become free, will never find their purpose, because they have what I call "the golden handcuffs." They make a little bit less money than it takes for them to survive. Their boss pays them enough to keep them there and they work just hard enough to keep from getting fired. So they are not going forward in life financially. They are too tired when they come home from work to see all of the opportunities before them.

They never can really become free. They can never drive the car they want or live the lifestyle they want. They can never have the income they want, but they are paralyzed by a paycheck and can't even think about a business opportunity. They can't even think about becoming wealthy because all they know is, "I gotta go to work for money." They are paralyzed by a paycheck. If you want to avoid this trap, build a business part time while you make a living at your job. When your income from your business is twice the amount you make on your job, you can be free of your golden handcuffs.

Practical Treasure Trap #6
We Do Everything Ourselves
We don't leverage our time by outsourcing things that we could pay someone else to do. If your time is worth $1000.00 per hour and you spend an hour washing your car, you just blew $1000.00. You could have paid someone else $10 to $50 to wash your car and you would have saved at least $950.00. If you take an

hour out of your day to ship out packages, you just blew another $1000.00. Don't use your valuable time doing menial tasks. Pay someone else for that. Once you get your business started, start outsourcing tasks as soon as you can. You want to spend more time working on your business (making it grow) than you do working in your business. Hire an assistant as soon you can afford to (which is sooner than you think). Pay someone to cut the grass, and clean the house and pick up your dry cleaning. Don't waste any of your valuable time doing trivial, menial tasks. In other words, don't step over a dollar to pick up a penny. You will see your income begin to multiply when you apply this principle.

Practical Treasure Trap #7
We Own the Wrong Kind of Business

Most of the time when an African-American starts a business, we start a service-oriented business. Many, many times it's a janitorial service. When you start a service-oriented business, as I already pointed out, you limit your income because service requires time. If you sell a product, it doesn't require time. Or it requires the same amount of time to sell one product as it does to sell 100,000 of that same product. What I want you to do is make sure that you don't fall into the Treasure Trap of starting a service-oriented business instead of starting a product-oriented business.

Practical Treasure Trap #8
We Don't Have Good Money Management Practices

You're going to have good money management practices from now on because you've got the money management principle of millionaires: Get all you can, can all you get and your cans mean you can. I can't emphasize it enough—go get your cans.

Practical Treasure Trap #9:
We Operate On A Cash Basis

I hear people say all the time, "I don't use banks. I don't write checks. I don't use credit cards. I don't use debit cards. I only use cash." Well, I'm going to tell you something. That is ultimately costing you money, because there is so much in the business world that you cannot do with cash. There is so much technology that you cannot take advantage of because you operate on a cash-only basis.

Open a savings account. Open a checking account. Get a debit card or get a credit card, or both. Stop operating only out of your pocket and with money that you keep under your mattress. Don't operate on a cash-only basis.

That is a Practical Treasure Trap because we don't want to focus on the details of balancing our checkbook when we write a check, and we end up bouncing checks. Then we get mad at the bank when it's really our fault. The checking account isn't the problem—not managing our money and not taking care of our financial business is. Take more responsibility and stop operating on a cash-only basis.

Practical Treasure Trap #10
We Don't Have a Financial Mentor or Coach

Folks, I cannot stress strongly enough the value of having a financial mentor who is doing better than you are.

Financial mentors stretch your thinking. They challenge you to go to another level. They hold you accountable for things that you won't hold yourself accountable for. Find a financial mentor or hire a financial coach because if you don't, you will miss a lot of opportunities.

The reason people have coaches, the reason people have mentors, is because you can't see the game when you're in the game. All you can see is what you can see. You need someone who is farther away from you, who can see the entire playing field. Who can see the entire game? Who can see what must be done in order to win? That is what you must have in your financial arena. Just like a basketball player, needs a coach on the basketball court. Or a football player needs one on the football field. Don't fall into the trap of not having a mentor.

Practical Treasure Trap #11
We Don't Set A Good Financial Example for Our Children

What a tragedy it is for parents not to be the best financial example that our children have. I believe one of the reasons our young people go down so many wrong roads is because we have set such a poor financial example for them. If the only people they see who are making money are people are doing something illegal, then they will be more tempted to go down that road.

Our young people have their dreams. They haven't gotten kicked around yet. They believe that their life is supposed to be good. Yet all they hear from their parents and other adults is that money doesn't grow on trees. "What do you think I am, made of money?" "What do you think my name is, Rockefeller?"

We've got to set a good financial example for our children. We've got to be our children's financial hero so they can know that there's hope for them. Create a legacy for your family, set a good example for your children.

Practical Treasure Trap #12
We Don't Teach Our Children How To Become Financially Free

We don't teach our children the principles that are in this book. One of the reasons I kept this book so simple is because I want you to be able to teach all of the principles in this book to your children. Anybody reading this book right now who has children who are in fifth grade or older, those children can understand these principles.

I urge you to take time to teach your children how money works and how to become financially independent. The lessons that you teach your children about money will save you and them a lot of heartache down the road.

Practical Treasure Trap #13
We Don't Use Good Debt; We Only Use Bad Debt

You may be wondering, "What is the difference between good debt and bad debt?" I like what Robert

Kiyosaki says, "Good debt is any money that you borrow and somebody else pays back. Bad debt is any money that you borrow that you pay back."

I'm going to make a recommendation to you, folks. When you borrow money for anything, create an asset, develop an asset, or buy an asset that pays off the debt from your purchase. Let me give you an example.

If you buy a house that's an investment property and your mortgage on that house is $500 a month and you rent that house out for $800 a month, somebody else is paying that debt back for you and you're generating cash flow at the same time. That's called good debt.

Bad debt is when you go buy a new car and you go to work at your job and you pay off that new car with the money you make from your job. That is bad debt. If you want to buy a new car, start an asset or create an asset that pays for that car.

You buy a car and your car payment is $300 a month. Go buy a piece of real estate where your mortgage is $500 a month and you rent it out for $800-$900 a month. Then your tenant pays for the new house you bought and the new car. That's called good debt.

You want to buy a new car? Go get involved with a Network Marketing company that has a car bonus program. Build your business up to the point where you can qualify for that new car and have the company pay for that car for you. That's good debt. You bought the car and the company pays for the car. You borrowed the money for the car and the company pays off the debt.

The Ebony Treasure Map

There are many, many different ways to use good debt instead of bad debt. The financial trap that we fall into is using bad debt instead of good debt.

CHAPTER SIXTEEN

How to Get Started On the Road to Riches

  This book is filled with page after page of powerful principles that can drastically change your financial life. You won't get rich overnight, but when you follow the path of the Ebony Treasure Map—changing the way you view and use money—you will soon be playing with the millionaires.

  I didn't write this book because I want you to *know* this information. I wrote this book because I want you to *do* this information. Start practicing the advice in this book today. Invest in self-education. Study what rich people do and what poor people do. Stop trading your time for money. Follow the advice of the rich and not the poor. Find a business that works with my hands-free marketing plan. And don't forget to avoid the treasure traps that will prevent you from reaching financial freedom.

  When you take these steps, you'll no longer be working just to "get by". You'll be thriving. You'll have plenty of money to take care of your bills, tithe, invest, and spend on yourself. You'll no longer be spending your time doing things you have to do. Instead, you'll be able to do the things you want to do, like play golf, or vacation in the tropics, or spend more time with your family.

  But let's keep first things first. Talk with the person who gave you this book and ask them what business they're in and if they can help you get started in it. If you bought this book from a retail store, online,

The Ebony Treasure Map

or if the person who recommended it to you doesn't have a business, then call our office and we will connect you with a mentor who can assist you in starting a product-oriented business that will be profitable for you. So I am going to finish this book by giving you some bonuses that will assist you in getting started on this great journey of financial independence. The bonuses that I am going to give you are worth over $3000.00 in value. So make sure you take advantage of them.

Here they are:

1. Two free tuitions to my two-day Six Figure Business School: a $2590.00 value, they're $1295 each. We have them all over the country. All you have to do is show the book to get in. Go to www.sixfigurebusinessschool.com to register for one of these national events.

2. One 15-minute coaching session with me or one of my Certified Prosperity Coaches (this session can be used to help you start a business or to help you grow a business that you already have). Just get back with the person you got this book from ore call our office and set up an appointment. 877-655-5663

3. An audio program on mp3 on the BEST Way To A Financial Turn Around.

I know when you take advantage of these bonuses; you will be well on your way to financial freedom. I am looking forward to seeing you at one of the Six Figure Business Schools somewhere across the country, or at one of our Ebony Treasure Map Evening events.

4. If you have found this book helpful to you, please call our toll-free testimonial line and leave a

testimony. Please understand that if you leave a testimony that it may be used in some of our marketing materials such as websites, brochures emails etc. If you do not want your testimonial used in this way then please don't leave one.

Toll-free testimonial line 1-800-604-4006 pin 218-0409 When you dial this number and pin it will prompt you to press 1 to record a message. After you record your message you will need to leave 3 seconds of silence and then it will prompt you to save or re-record.

Your life is about to change for the better. Enjoy the ride.

About The Author

Myron Golden is a dynamic trainer and international speaker with over 19 years of experience in the business development, marketing, and sales arenas. He has on the same platform with such well-known speakers as Les Brown, Jerry Clark, Jim Rohn, Wade B. Cook and Mark Victor Hansen.

Myron knows that it's easier to make a lot of money than it is to make a little bit. He empowers others by teaching them the three ways to grow a business, the three functions of business, how to earn money by generating leads for their businesses, and why you have no competition in business.

More than just a "feel good" motivator, Myron gives specific "How To" and "What To" instruction on the topics of internet marketing, business development, sales, Network Marketing and lead generation. Those who hear him are immediately able to utilize his techniques to help them reach their goals.

Twenty years ago Myron was a trash man. Now he's a cash man. The owner of several independent businesses, he now produces six-figure monthly, weekly and even daily results. In The Ebony Treasure Map, Myron shares his story and teaches other African Americans how to change the way they view (and use) money.

Myron lives in Pennsylvania with his wife and three children.